# INFINITE GRACE

## THE DEVOTIONAL

Patsy Clairmont    Mary Graham

Nicole Johnson    Carol Kent    Marilyn Meberg

Sandi Patty    Jan Silvious    Luci Swindoll

Sheila Walsh    Thelma Wells

THOMAS NELSON
*Since 1798*

NASHVILLE   DALLAS   MEXICO CITY   RIO DE JANEIRO

Infinite Grace: The Devotional
© 2008 Patsy Clairmont, Mary Graham, Nicole Johnson, Carol Kent, Marilyn Meberg, Sandi Patty, Jan Silvious, Luci Swindoll, Sheila Walsh, Thelma Wells

Published in Nashville, Tennessee, by Thomas Nelson. Thomas Nelson is a registered trademark of Thomas Nelson, Inc.

Thomas Nelson, Inc. titles may be purchased in bulk for educational, business, fund-raising, or sales promotional use. For information, please e-mail SpecialMarkets@ThomasNelson.com.

Some names and identifying details have been changed to protect the privacy of the individuals involved.

Scripture quotations are taken from the following versions: The New Century Version® (NCV). Copyright © 1987, 1988, 1991 by Thomas Nelson, Inc. Used by permission. All rights reserved. The Message (MSG) by Eugene H. Peterson. Copyright © 1993, 1994, 1995, 1996, 2000, 2001, 2002. Used by permission of NavPress Publishing Group. All rights reserved. The New King James Version® (NKJV®). Copyright © 1982 by Thomas Nelson, Inc. Used by permission. All rights reserved. The Holy Bible, New International Version® (NIV®). Copyright © 1973, 1978, 1984 by International Bible Society. Used by permission of Zondervan. All rights reserved. The Holy Bible, New Living Translation® (NLT®). Copyright © 1996, 2004. Used by permission of Tyndale House Publishers, Inc., Wheaton, Illinois 60189. All rights reserved. The New American Standard Bible® (NASB®). Copyright © 1960, 1962, 1963, 1968, 1971, 1972, 1973, 1975, 1977, 1995 by The Lockman Foundation. Used by permission. The King James Version of the Bible (KJV). Public domain.

Cover Design: Brand Navigation
Interior Design: Lori Lynch, Book & Graphic Design, Nashville, TN

ISBN 978-1-4002-7818-3 (TP)
ISBN 978-0-8499-1955-8

Printed in the United States of America
10 11 12 13 LSI 6 5 4 3 2 1

In loving memory
of Barbara Johnson

# Contents

BOUNDLESS GRACE

1. Grace That Knows No Limits—*Sheila Walsh* . . . . . . . . . 1
2. A God Like This—*Thelma Wells* . . . . . . . . . . . . . . . . . 7
3. Flooded with Grace—*Mary Graham* . . . . . . . . . . . . . 12
4. God's Photo Album of Grace—*Nicole Johnson* . . . . . . 18
5. A Dog Named Grace—*Jan Silvious* . . . . . . . . . . . . . . 23
6. Off Your Rocker—*Luci Swindoll* . . . . . . . . . . . . . . . . 28
7. An Unexpected Companion—*Carol Kent* . . . . . . . . . . . 34
8. Grace and Character Building—*Marilyn Meberg* . . . . . . 41
9. All-Star Grace—*Sandi Patty* . . . . . . . . . . . . . . . . . . . 47
10. Make Space for Grace—*Patsy Clairmont* . . . . . . . . . . 52

UNFATHOMABLE GRACE

11. Dad's Final Flight—*Carol Kent* . . . . . . . . . . . . . . . . . 61
12. Glimpses of Grace—*Marilyn Meberg* . . . . . . . . . . . . . 67
13. Out of Egypt—*Luci Swindoll* . . . . . . . . . . . . . . . . . . 73
14. Available Grace—*Sandi Patty* . . . . . . . . . . . . . . . . . . 79
15. Always Welcomed Home—*Sheila Walsh* . . . . . . . . . . . 84
16. Words of Grace—*Patsy Clairmont* . . . . . . . . . . . . . . . 90
17. Quiet Grace—*Nicole Johnson* . . . . . . . . . . . . . . . . . . 96
18. Amazing Grace—*Mary Graham* . . . . . . . . . . . . . . . . 101
19. Mindful of Grace—*Thelma Wells* . . . . . . . . . . . . . . . 107
20. Grace Walking—*Jan Silvious* . . . . . . . . . . . . . . . . . . 113

## IMMEASURABLE GRACE

21. Missing Grace—*Nicole Johnson* . . . . . . . . . . . . . . . 121
22. Measuring Up—*Patsy Clairmont* . . . . . . . . . . . . . . . 127
23. A Matter of Perspective—*Carol Kent* . . . . . . . . . . . . 133
24. An Unending Supply—*Sheila Walsh* . . . . . . . . . . . . 139
25. Grace: Fullness of Life—*Marilyn Meberg* . . . . . . . . . 145
26. Many-Colored Grace—*Jan Silvious* . . . . . . . . . . . . . 151
27. Nudges of Grace—*Luci Swindoll* . . . . . . . . . . . . . . . 156
28. He Giveth More Grace—*Mary Graham* . . . . . . . . . . . 162
29. Resting in Grace—*Sandi Patty* . . . . . . . . . . . . . . . . 168
30. Refining Grace—*Thelma Wells* . . . . . . . . . . . . . . . . 171

## ETERNAL GRACE

31. Forever Grace—*Patsy Clairmont* . . . . . . . . . . . . . . . 179
32. Grace Beyond Rules—*Jan Silvious* . . . . . . . . . . . . . . 185
33. Grace for All People—*Mary Graham* . . . . . . . . . . . . 191
34. Sheltering Grace—*Marilyn Meberg* . . . . . . . . . . . . . 197
35. Grace Greater Than Our Sin—*Nicole Johnson* . . . . . . 203
36. Marker Moments—*Carol Kent* . . . . . . . . . . . . . . . . 209
37. Grace in Sickness and Death—*Thelma Wells* . . . . . . . 215
38. Grace for Eternity—*Sandi Patty* . . . . . . . . . . . . . . . 221
39. Mutual Grace—*Luci Swindoll* . . . . . . . . . . . . . . . . . 226
40. Grasp This Moment!—*Sheila Walsh* . . . . . . . . . . . . 232

## IN MEMORY OF BARBARA JOHNSON

41. Barbara Johnson—*Mary Graham* . . . . . . . . . . . . . . . 239

42. Dear Barbara—*Patsy Clairmont* . . . . . . . . . . . . . . . . . 244
43. Barbara Johnson—*Marilyn Meberg* . . . . . . . . . . . . . 249
44. The Unforgettable Barbara Johnson—*Luci Swindoll* . . . 253

*Notes* . . . . . . . . . . . . . . . . . . . . . . . . . . . . . . . . . . . . . 259

# BOUNDLESS
# GRACE

1

# Grace That Knows No Limits

~ Sheila Walsh ~

The next day as the three travelers were approaching the town, Peter went out on the balcony to pray. It was about noon. Peter got hungry and started thinking about lunch. While lunch was being prepared, he fell into a trance. He saw the skies open up. Something that looked like a huge blanket lowered by ropes at its four corners settled on the ground. Every kind of animal and reptile and bird you could think of was on it. Then a voice came: "Go to it, Peter—kill and eat." Peter said, "Oh, no, Lord. I've never so much as tasted food that was not kosher." The voice came a second time: "If God says it's okay, it's okay."

—Acts 10:9–15 MSG

When our son, Christian, was seven years old, he announced to his dad and me that he *needed* a dog. I was impressed with his choice of verb. As a child I told my mom that I wanted a dog and never got one. I now realize that it might have been as simple as my misuse of the English language! When I asked Christian why he needed a dog, his explanation made total sense to me. "Mom, I am an only child. I need someone to talk to." I reminded him that he had his dad and me to talk to, but Christian wisely replied, "No, I need someone to talk to about you."

So after some careful research, we added Belle to our family. Belle is a beautiful bichon frise with the huge plus that she does not shed. I used to have a golden retriever, and I could have stuffed cushions with the amount of fur he cast off daily.

Almost three years later, Christian announced that he was concerned about Belle. She seemed fine to me—perhaps a little overweight, but hey, I had no stones to throw. I asked him what he thought her problem was. "She's lonely," he said. "There's nothing worse than a lonely bichon." So Tink was added to our motley crew. She too is a bichon frise but from the French line as opposed to the American. Her fur is longer and silkier, yet it stays firmly attached to her frame, so all is well.

As far as I could tell, we were done. Belle no longer required therapy, and she and Tink get along fairly well. Like children they have very different personalities. Belle lives to please me, and Tink dances to the beat of "Wild Thing!" Peace appeared to reign, but life was about to take an unexpected twist in the road.

I was sitting in the departure lounge at Little Rock airport. The other Women of Faith speakers and I had just finished our first conference of 2007, and we were all exhausted. Most weekends we can't get a flight back to Dallas until Sunday morning, but we had all been able to get on the last flight out on Saturday night.

I was sitting on the floor talking to Luci when my cell phone rang. It was Christian. It was a poor connection, and I could only make out snippets of what he was saying. It sounded something like this: "Pet store . . . Shivering . . . Poor dog . . . Dad said if you said . . . Mom?"

I have no idea what I mumbled, but the minute I sat down on the plane, the picture became alarmingly clear. I hurriedly sent a text message to my husband, Barry: *Please tell me we don't have another dog!*

The reply came back: *Yes we do, and his name is Trevor.*

I quickly typed: *What is he?*

The response was: *He is a Wiener dog!*

My first thought of panic was replaced by a fond memory. When I was a little girl my father bought me a Wiener dog, but after my father became ill we had to get rid of her. *Perhaps God is giving me back what I lost,* I mused to myself in a sleep-deprived haze. Then I got home!

Whatever Trevor is, the word *Wiener* does not accurately describe his size. *Salami* perhaps, but not Wiener. He looks as if he is 10 percent Wiener and 90 percent Rottweiler. His paws are the size of dinner plates. After my initial shock at Trevor's unusual appearance, what was interesting to me was how Belle and Tink responded to him. They are very friendly dogs and normally love to meet up with dogs of all shapes and sizes, but they definitely gave Trevor the cold shoulder. They walked around him once or twice and then with a shake of their perfectly groomed heads left him in their dust. I hate to say it, but I have two bichon snobs—prejudiced pooches.

Two of the first sins of the fall of Adam and Eve were prejudice and separation. Adam blamed Eve, and Eve blamed the serpent. But the sin was more pronounced in their sons, Cain and Abel. When Cain compared himself to Abel and saw that God showed favor on Abel's offering and not on his, hatred began to grow inside him like a cancer. And like many cancers, Cain's hatred led to death—not his own, but the murder of his brother Abel.

There is something in our sinful brokenness that wants to compare ourselves to others and say who gets to be "in" and who is left out in the cold. Trevor received no points from the bichon frise judges, just as the Gentiles received no points from the Jews. During the time of Christ, there was no love lost between the Jews and the Gentiles. In some rabbinical writings, devout Jews actually believed that God allowed Gentiles to be born to fuel the fires of hell. Jews referred to Gentiles as "dogs." But because of the boundless grace of God, that was all about to change.

Peter was a changed man after the resurrection of Christ. He was bold and fearless as he shared the good news that

Messiah had come and there was forgiveness of sins. He set out on a mission trip with John and saw God perform many miracles. Peter and John traveled to Samaria to join Phillip in the revival happening there, and in Joppa he saw Dorcas brought back from the dead. But God was about to prepare Peter for a whole new world.

In Caesarea lived an Italian centurion named Cornelius who feared God. One day an angel appeared to him and told him that God, in his boundless grace, saw Cornelius's heart and had answered his prayers. The angel told Cornelius to send for a man named Peter who was staying with Simon the tanner. At the same time as this was taking place in Caesarea, Peter was watching a movie sent from God on a rooftop by the sea in Joppa. In this vision Peter was asked to eat food that a devout Jew would never touch. The voice in Peter's vision told him that if God says this is okay, then it's okay. By the time Cornelius's messenger made it to Peter, the apostle's heart was ready to accept the invitation to come to Caesarea and share the gospel with the Gentiles.

God's boundless grace has no room for prejudice. Every man, woman, and child is made and loved by God. He sees no distinction between races and colors, wealth and poverty, the cultured and the coarse. I see no greater challenge extended to the church today than this: to share the boundless grace of God that knows no limits to everyone we meet.

Now, how do I get that across to Belle and Tink?

✿ ✿ ✿

*Lord, I admit that sometimes I turn a cold shoulder to people who aren't like me. Help me to view others the way you see them—as your precious and beloved creations. And give me opportunities today to share your boundless, limitless grace with everyone I meet. Amen.*

# 2

# A God Like This

## ~ Thelma Wells ~

O LORD, You have searched me and known me.
You know my sitting down and my rising up;
You understand my thought afar off.
You comprehend my path and my lying down,
And are acquainted with all my ways. . . .

For You formed my inward parts;
You covered me in my mother's womb.
I will praise You, for I am fearfully and wonderfully made;
Marvelous are Your works,
And that my soul knows very well.
My frame was not hidden from You,
When I was made in secret,
And skillfully wrought in the lowest parts of the earth.
Your eyes saw my substance, being yet unformed.
And in Your book they all were written,
The days fashioned for me,
When as yet there were none of them. . . .

Search me, O God, and know my heart;
Try me, and know my anxieties;

And see if there is any wicked way in me,
And lead me in the way everlasting.

—Psalm 139:1–3, 13–16, 23–24 NKJV

When I think about the goodness of Jesus and everything he's done for me, my soul exclaims, "Hallelujah!" I thank God for blessing me. When I read David's words in Psalm 139, I am amazed.

Now, y'all, tell me, if this psalm is not a perfect example of God's infinite grace, I don't know what it is. This is the boundless, unlimited, unsurpassed, ever present, everlasting, ever fulfilling, ever sustaining grace of God.

Do you hear David declaring that God knows all about us? He knows our weaknesses and our strengths, our sins and our sainthood, our ups and our downs, our thoughts and our ways. Even though God knows us better than ourselves, he does not condemn those who have accepted his son as the Savior. Romans 8:1 assures us that there is no condemnation to those who love the Lord. This is favor from God that we don't deserve and have no control over. God gives it freely by his boundless grace toward us.

God is everywhere, all the time, in every situation, watching over us, protecting us, correcting us, covering us under his wings of guardianship as a ward of the kingdom of God. We can trust God when life is so difficult we cannot hear the march of any other drum major giving orders for our direction. When all hell breaks out in our situations and we feel like things will never end, we are held up by the boundless, matchless Spirit of God who leads us to the dawn of a new day.

There is nowhere on earth we can go that God is not there. Remember, "The earth is the Lord's, and all its fullness, the world and those who dwell therein" (Psalm 24:1 NKJV). This ever-watching grace of God was here before the foundation of the world and was personified at the birth of Jesus Christ when grace took on flesh and dwelled among us. It was grace that brought us safe this far, and grace will lead us home. Infinite, boundless grace!

When David talks about how God made us, I picture in my mind that God, before the foundation of the world, before he separated the expanse from the earth, had a holy warehouse with our names on each cubicle, and he had already decided when we would be born and to whom we would be born. He knew all our life's mountains and valleys and how we would respond to each. In spite of knowing all about us, he lovingly and inexplicably formed us with his power to live in a world of decay and unrighteousness with the ability of our bodies to heal themselves, with our limbs to move on their own, with the ability to speak and be understood, with the resources to earn a living, with the humanity to care for others, with the desire to know him and to return to our Father, who made us. (Okay, let's stop! I'm about to shout now!)

He knew we would go through dangers, toils, and snares and would not have a clue how to work them out for ourselves. And in spite of our neglect of our bodies, minds, and spirits, he made us in his spiritual image and gave us the human ability to understand a smattering of the love of God. This is God's boundless, infinite grace.

God extends his unmerited favor to everyone who will receive, no matter what we have done. I guess that may be one reason it is boundless. His boundless grace covers everybody, everywhere in the universe. So when you get ready to ask God to do harm to your enemy, think about how you've done things you should not have done and said things you should not have said. God covered your sin with his unlimited grace. He loves other people just like he loves you. Even when you think of yourself more highly than you ought, God shows you that his grace is sufficient to help you get up when you fall down.

As they say in my church, "Who wouldn't serve a God like this?" A God who picks you up when you call, who made you in his spiritual image, a God who is with you every day in every way, a God who knows more about you than you do yourself, a God who grants you something you can't see, taste, smell, hear, or touch—you just know his grace has to be there because the blessings of God keep coming and coming and coming even when you don't earn it and don't deserve it. That's nothing but the boundless, limitless, infinite grace of a true and living God.

✿ ✿ ✿

*Father God, in the name of your Son, Jesus, the grace giver, please search me, O God, and know my heart; try me, and know my anxieties. And see if there is any wicked way in me, and lead me in the way everlasting. Amen.*

# 3

# Flooded with Grace

~ Mary Graham ~

But now, this is what the LORD says—
he who created you, O Jacob,
   he who formed you, O Israel:
"Fear not, for I have redeemed you;
   I have summoned you by name; you are mine.
When you pass through the waters,
   I will be with you;
and when you pass through the rivers,
   they will not sweep over you. . . .
For I am the LORD, your God,
   the Holy One of Israel, your Savior.
            —Isaiah 43:1–3 NIV

Every now and then, we have an unforgettable encounter with grace. Such a thing happened to me a few months ago when I was visiting in the Hill Country of Texas. My memorable moment was with the hotel's maid . . . actually, she was the supervisor of the maids.

I was standing almost in the doorway of my room when

Geraldine, the maid who dropped by to replace a coffeepot, started telling me her story. I casually greeted her and thanked her for her service. I don't remember how we began our long conversation, but she had me at the mention of the name Katrina.

As her story unfolded, I found myself in tears. Geraldine had been serving as a maid with a hotel company in New Orleans when Hurricane Katrina hit. The national chain was completely full of guests when the storm began to roll in. Many of those guests got in their cars and drove away from the storm, but those who were far from home or too scared to travel decided to wait in the safety of this plush, five-star, nationally known and highly acclaimed hotel. How could anything happen to them if they were safely tucked away in such luxury and protected from the storm?

The hotel's manager asked the staff to stay at the hotel, serving the guests. The request seemed reasonable at first, but as the hours and then days wore on, the weather got worse outside and tensions held sway inside.

By the second day of the impending storm warning, with a hotel full of guests, it was apparent real trouble was on the way. The manager said to his staff, "If you'll stay here and take care of the guests, we'll take care of you." Geraldine called for her daughter and granddaughter to come to the hotel, knowing they wouldn't be safe at home.

When the levies broke, the hotel lobby began to flood.

All of the guests stepped into large garbage bags from their feet to their waists and were literally floated by the staff to the front door and down to a bus, where they were taken to Baton Rouge.

After the guests were safe, the staff members were removed to Baton Rouge as well. That city was already inundated with refugees, so finding a place to house the hotel guests was challenging. One hotel, a sister of the New Orleans chain, refused. The Baton Rouge manager phoned the corporate headquarters in another state and was told, "If you don't take care of these guests, our name is coming off your building."

Again the staff was reminded, "If you take care of the guests, we'll take care of you." Arrangements were finally made for the guests to return safely to their homes, but the staff members were stuck. They had no homes, no hotels, and no jobs to go home to. New Orleans was a wreck, and so were they.

So the manager said to the staff, "Here are all the cities where our corporation has hotels. Choose a place you'd like to go, and we will fly you there with your family, guarantee you a job, and help you get settled."

For Geraldine, this was being rescued not just from the storm but from a life of difficulty in the city where she'd grown up but had never found the right opportunity to excel. Geraldine, her daughter, and grandchild needed a new beginning, but how in the world could that ever happen on her meager salary?

Geraldine chose Texas. She'd always wanted to live in Texas because it seemed like a friendly place. The hotel chain gave her a permanent position, a place to live at least temporarily, and everything she needed to get started. The first weekend in her new home state, she found a church. She said she was terrified to discover when she walked in the church that she was the only nonwhite face in the crowd. However, it didn't take long to realize that didn't matter.

She was embraced by the congregation and the pastor. He introduced her in the service and by the time she said good-bye to him that morning, she had a car loaned to her, a promise of a permanent place to live, and everything she needed to set up her new life in Texas. "Boy, these Texans!" she said to me again and again.

The Monday following that service, someone she'd met at church took her to a car dealer and helped her to get a car. While she was there, she spotted a young man she knew from the hotel in New Orleans. She asked how he was doing, and he said OK but he needed a car to get to work. The car dealer asked the boy how much money he had. Embarrassed, the young man responded, "About a dollar." The dealer then said, "How about that car over there? Do you like it?" When the young man nodded, here's what he heard: "I can sell you that car for about a dollar."

I stood there in the doorway of my hotel room, holding the coffeepot and blinking away tears as I listened to Geraldine go on and on and on with stories like this. She praised the hotel chain, the people, the church, the pastor, the car dealer, the butcher, the baker, the candlestick maker. But mostly she praised God.

What I was hearing was not just a story of goodness; it was a remarkable story of grace. My dear friend and mentor, Dr. Bill Bright, always said, "A life of grace leads to gratitude." Geraldine was full of gratitude. She had been delivered, and she was deeply thankful. God had done something for her through an unusual chain of events that she'd longed for but could not do for herself or her family.

It's so easy to limit God . . . to look at the circumstances of our lives and think, *This is impossible.* Or, *This will never work.* We cannot even imagine how our problems might be solved, how our angst could be abated or our fears calmed. So we worry. Yet God tells us to trust him to take care of the future we cannot see. I love the apostle Paul's encouraging words in Philippians 4:6: "Be anxious for nothing, but in everything by prayer and supplication with thanksgiving let your requests be made known to God" (NASB).

I used to think that was simply a command I needed to obey. But as I get older and hear more stories like Geraldine's and see how my own life story unfolds, I see the verse differently. The real reason we should not be anxious is not merely because it's a command (although I suppose my mother would tell me that is reason enough!), but because God really is in control. He really does take care of us. His grace *is* sufficient (and then some!).

Even through the storms of life, God has his ways of pouring out his boundless grace on even seemingly impossible circumstances. Just ask Geraldine.

✻ ✻ ✻

*Lord, thank you for your boundless grace, which keeps the storms of life from drowning my hope. No matter how difficult my circumstances may be, I will look to you to pour out your grace and rain down your all-sufficient love and care for me. Amen.*

# 4

# God's Photo Album of Grace

~ Nicole Johnson ~

Then He said, "To what shall we liken the kingdom of God?
Or with what parable shall we picture it?"

—Mark 4:30 NKJV

I've been spending a lot of time in photo albums lately.

Just a few short weeks ago, we welcomed a firstborn son into our family, and the shutter on our camera has been clicking like crazy ever since. We've tried to capture his time in the hospital, his arrival home, his first nap in his bassinet, what he looks like on Tuesdays—all the silly photos parents take when they are utterly smitten with a new baby. Soon I'll have to find the time (aka make the time) to arrange them in a book that will forever remind us of these days.

When I turned forty last December, my parents thought it was a good time to return all my childhood photos to me. But what they did was return them in beautiful album form. Pages and pages, lovingly created to showcase everything from my baby pictures to awkward junior high moments through high school dances and on to college. So many memories came flooding back through their incredible gift to me.

I've also been working on a photo album of our extended family. Both of my husband's parents have passed away, and we feel a strong desire to help our son know them even though they aren't here to participate in his life. We'll bring them into his world through photos and stories and reliving memories to try to create an accurate picture of their lives and their contribution to his life, even though he can't see them. It is so important to us that our son knows his heritage and the family on his father's side.

And this is important to me as a believer as well—that I know my heritage and the family on my Father's side. What is the Bible if it isn't God's photo album? It's a book full of our heritage, with pictures of the infinite love, mercy, favor, and goodwill shown to humankind by God. So often we just reduce the Bible to some set of principles, or we focus only on its doctrine—but it's a beautiful album featuring living pictures of God's grace. I learn so much about who he is and what he is about by studying his album.

If we take some time to flip through the pages, we can see some of the photos:

Like in the book of Genesis, where we find Noah building an ark on his front lawn, much to the chagrin of his neighbors . . . a picture of the peace that God wanted to offer to mankind.

And then, a few chapters later, we see the joyful picture of God giving Sarah a child called Laughter when she was ninety years old.

In Luke 15, we find a picture of a prodigal son that gives us a glimpse of the loving heart of God.

Then we see the woman caught in adultery about to be stoned. What a portrait of grace—the way Christ stands between us and our accusers.

And then we see the woman with the issue of blood—remember how she just tried to touch the hem of his garment without anyone seeing her? What a picture of his gentle healing.

What about the time Jesus was in the temple and he healed a man with a withered hand—showing us how to go against the Pharisees when their religion had replaced their love?

All four Gospels give us the picture of Jesus feeding of the five thousand—teaching us of his multiplication and constant provision.

And one of the greatest pictures of grace comes in the empty tomb, giving us the hope of the life eternal that he promised.

The pages go on and on. The stories, the snapshots of God's grace. This is how we come to know of God and his love for us, through pictures of all he has done.

Before the first Bible was printed, these word pictures were the only way people could learn about God. In fact, stained-glass windows in cathedrals were designed with images that represented the life and work of Christ, created to tell the gospel story so people could see it.

Pictures and photo albums are powerful tools. Photographs have a way of getting into our minds and sticking there like little Post-it notes in our brains. Marriage experts have reported that couples who keep photo albums of their memories have healthier relationships and are actually less likely to divorce. I wonder if that's because they spend more time remembering and reflecting on their history together and relishing the great moments. They keep falling in love all over again.

Flipping through the pages of God's Word when we see it as his photo album of grace is much the same thing. As we turn the pages, we remember the amazing things he's done, and our relationship with him grows and deepens. We remember and reflect on our history with him, and we relish the great moments. We see clearly his faithfulness and his provision for us, and we love and trust him all over again.

Many people keep a journal of some sort to record their prayer requests as well as the answers they receive. It's a very personal way to flip through the pages of your history to see God's grace and remember his faithfulness. It's so easy to forget or take for granted all that he has done. I am always humbled and grateful when I look back through my journal.

One day, I'll look back on my son's first photo album that I'm creating and I'll marvel at how far he's come. I'll remember these days of not sleeping, and I will thank God for getting us through. Then I'll open the other albums and show our son pictures of the grandparents he won't have the privilege to know. But I'll tell him stories about them so he can understand who they are and what they mean to us.

And right along with it, I'll open God's photo album. I'll point to the photos of grace and help him come to understand who God is and what he means to us and, most importantly, who God can be in his life.

✳ ✳ ✳

*Father, continue to show us how to look at your Word like a photo album of your grace. Burn the pictures of your faithfulness into our minds so when the doubts come, as they will, we can see clearly how you provide. Give us wisdom as we seek to show others pictures of your grace and love. And as we remember all you have done for us in your infinite grace, our hearts will return your amazing love. Amen.*

# 5

# A Dog Named Grace

~ Jan Silvious ~

For the Son of Man came to seek and save those who are lost.

—Luke 19:10 NLT

I believe God speaks to us in ways we can understand. We have his written Word, the Bible, and we have his sweet Holy Spirit, who occupies the mind and heart of every believer with counsel, comfort, and truth. These are God's basic tools of communication to his children. But he also allows circumstances, people, and yes, even creatures to cross our paths and give us living demonstrations of what he wants us to know. In my life, he used an orphaned dog to speak to my heart many wonderful truths about grace.

She came into our lives on a cold February day—a black Lab puppy abandoned at a park where my husband regularly jogged. When my husband jogged by where she was playing, she ran out and nipped at his heels. Knowing the night was going to be frigid and having a tender heart toward helpless creatures, he brought her home. We tried to find a home for her, but I can honestly say I didn't try too hard because when our eyes met, we bonded. So when it looked as if the puppy was going to join our family, I decided to give her a name that would be consistent with our other dog. (It's a girl thing, you know, to match up the names!)

Our other dog's name was Mercy. She was an elderly poodle who was very self-possessed and had already relegated me to *persona non grata*. Mercy had her favorites, and trust me, I wasn't one of them. Any stranger who came to the house got more attention than I did. Mercy was set in her ways and didn't care what anyone thought, least of all me!

Wanting to have a little redemptive reasoning in the naming of the new puppy, I thought, *Why not call her Grace?* I had great hopes that her name would fit her far better than "Mercy" suited our little Tasmanian devil in the poodle suit! We would have Mercy and Grace—it was perfect.

And so our lives together began. There were lessons we learned from Grace that only could have been taught through an animal who had no idea she was a living demonstration of greater truths.

It was soon apparent that Grace was going to be a very big girl, so I enrolled her in a training class. The first night, I realized that the other twenty-five dogs in our group were pedigreed! Yep, Grace and I were the only strays in this class. We felt the haughtiness in the gaze of the other dogs and owners, but that was OK. Grace and I had each other, and we had a goal. We passed the first week's lesson—*sit*. She mastered that with brilliance. The second week was *stay*. Again, she wowed me and I can only assume the other owners with her quick completion of the instructions. We were on a roll! I was proud of her, and I think she probably was very proud of herself.

The third week of dog training classes came, and Grace and I were ready. Whatever the instructor threw at us, we knew we could handle it. Not only was she to *sit* and *stay*, but she was to do so while I walked away from her. All the other dogs were sitting and staying with great intensity—until Grace lost sight of me. She just couldn't stand it. She broke out of her *stay* command and ran to find me. When she did, the twenty-five other pedigreed dogs took their cue from her, the wayward stray. Owners, dogs, leashes, and instructor were all in upheaval. The circle was broken, the dogs were awry, and I thought, *Oh no, what has happened here!*

At that moment, I looked down and saw my Grace, sitting at my feet in perfect form. She had found me, and she was sitting and staying. All she had wanted was me. Despite the barking chaos around us, I leaned down and whispered in Grace's ear, "Good girl." She had found me and had no intention of leaving my side. That was all I wanted from her.

Later, I thought of all the times I messed up in something I was supposed to be learning, and yet God drew me up close to himself and said, *Good girl. Stay close to me, and we will work it all out.* That really is a picture of grace. Grace is not earned, nor is it anything we can do for ourselves. It is solely based on the heart of the Father, who always seeks his own.

God isn't looking for the pedigreed who have no need. He is looking for the confused and lost who could never make it without him.

I love this scripture that speaks of God's heart full of grace demonstrated in his son, Jesus:

> Tax collectors and other notorious sinners often came to listen to Jesus teach. This made the Pharisees and teachers of religious law complain that he was associating with such sinful people—even eating with them!
>
> So Jesus told them this story: "If a man has a hundred sheep and one of them gets lost, what will he do? Won't he leave the ninety-nine others in the wilderness and go to search for the one that is lost until he finds it? And when he has found it, he will joyfully carry it home on his shoulders. When he arrives, he will call together his friends and neighbors, saying, 'Rejoice with me because I have found my lost sheep.' In the same way, there is more joy in heaven over one lost sinner who repents and returns to God than over ninety-nine others who are righteous and haven't strayed away!" (Luke 15:1–7 NLT)

God loves you just the way you are, and he will spare no effort to find you and get you home safely. That is his pure and wonderful grace!

☆ ☆ ☆

*Lord, thank you for seeking me and finding me when I was confused and lost. Today, I will come close to you so I can hear you say, "Good girl. Stay close to me, and we will work it all out." Amen.*

# 6

# Off Your Rocker

~ Luci Swindoll ~

Oh, how sweet the light of day,
And how wonderful to live in the sunshine!
Even if you live a long time, don't take a single day for granted.
Take delight in each light-filled hour.

—Ecclesiastes 11:7–8 MSG

ollywood has a new darling! Her name is Mae Laborde.
She has what *USA Today* calls "a fresh new face."[1] At the
age of ninety-seven, Ms. Laborde is just four years into an
enviable, exciting, and busy acting career . . . wrinkles and all.
At four feet ten inches, with snow white hair, she's in a
movie with Ben Stiller and proud of it. She took her first
casting call at ninety-three, which led to a Sears commercial;
then she appeared on *Mad TV*. Following that came ads for
Lexus automobiles and Chase Bank. The woman never stops!
She's been a cheerleader on ESPN and faced down the Grim
Reaper himself in a lighthearted bit about elderly people without health insurance for HBO's *Real Time with Bill Maher*.

Before her recent stardom, Mae Laborde worked as a bookkeeper in the late bandleader Lawrence Welk's office. But she always had a yen to act. In 2002, the *Los Angeles Times* ran a story about Ms. Laborde when columnist Steve Lopez saw her charging up and down Santa Monica's neighborhood streets and across the freeways in her gigantic 1977 Oldsmobile Delta 88. "She was so small and the car so big," Mr. Lopez wrote, "that behind the wheel she looked like a cricket driving a tank." His description caught the eye of an LA talent agent, Sherrie Spillane (former wife of Mickey Spillane), and when the two got together . . . Mae's dream started coming true! Sherrie Spillane got a new client, and Mae Laborde got a second childhood.

Life at any age is truly what we make it. My right knee hurts. Most of the time. Sometimes I also have pain in my right leg and the left knee. Arthritis. I think it's here to stay. I'm not yet a candidate for knee surgery, but one day I probably will be. The doctor says it has to get worse first.

When I read, my left eye has blurred vision. Most of the time. Sometimes it's in both eyes. Cataracts. I think they're here to stay. I'm not yet a candidate for cataract surgery, but one day I probably will be. The doctor says my vision has to get worse first.

When I bend over, my back aches. Most of the time. Sometimes it hurts in the lower back and occasionally in my shoulders. I think it's here to stay. I'm not a candidate for back surgery, but one day I probably will be. The doctor says nobody goes through life without some kind of back pain.

And then there's my mind. Occasionally it sort of fades. Nothing hurts, but I can't remember facts I used to carry around with the greatest of ease. And now I constantly ask myself: *Did I take my meds? Is today when I promised to feed my friend's cat? Have I dropped that letter in the mail? Where are my car keys?* I haven't seen a doctor about this nagging irritation, but one day I probably will. I'm not yet a candidate for a brain transplant.

Aging reminds me of that country-and-western song, "I've Enjoyed about as Much of This as I Can Stand."

In Victor Hugo's epic work *Les Miserables,* there's a wonderful line about aging. It reads, "When grace is joined with wrinkles, it is adorable. There is an unspeakable dawn in happy old age."[2] Before I get too old to think for myself, let's explore that concept of "an unspeakable dawn." What does it mean?

I believe it means finding the ability to start something new and fresh—enjoying a second childhood, pursuing a dream that was not possible before now. And I love that part where "grace is joined with wrinkles." The wrinkles won't go away, but grace makes them acceptable. We can endure anything when grace is present. Life is buoyant and creative and adorable . . . even in old age. For example, here's a start:

Fifteen days from now, I'm taking a cruise to the Greek Isles with my brother Chuck and his Insight for Living staff.

One hundred and sixty IFL listeners have signed up to go on a full-sail ship from Istanbul to Athens through the Eastern Aegean. I've been to Greece eight times and seen many of the islands, but not these particular ones. We'll be following the missionary journeys of the apostle Paul, with my brother Chuck speaking at every significant stop. I can't wait.

When I get back, I'll start right into a full travel schedule with Women of Faith.

In 2008, it's my plan to begin an in-depth reading program of the classics I never got to in college. I've written out a whole list.

And my landscaper and I have an idea of how I'll begin my own vegetable garden. I might plant it in an old wagon so I can roll it around the yard where it's convenient enough to work without having to bend over much or hobble on my arthritic leg. We'll figure it out.

I've got so many dreams I need to fit in with these bad knees, poor vision, sore back, and weakening mind—and I'm only seventy-five. But I'm asking God for the grace to do them all in my "happy old age."

Face it, Luci . . . aging is definitely here to stay; there's no way to get around it. Scripture tells us, "It is appointed unto men once to die" (Hebrews 9:27 KJV) . . . and I can promise you this: if you live your desired four score and twenty, you *will* age before you die. And a lot of how we age has to do with our attitude toward it.

When asked her secret for living a long life, Ms. Laborde tells people to never retire. And get this—at the age of eighty-nine, this spunky little lady took a police training course just for fun. She still cooks for herself, paints, and raises tomatoes in her garden and sells them to a local restaurant. And to those who never open the shades to their "unspeakable dawn," Mae Laborde says, "Get off your rocker and get out there and see what's going on!"[3] Go Mae! I wish you were my neighbor.

Oh, one more thing. Ms. Spillane wrote, "I don't know anyone else her age that could keep up with her. But then . . . I don't know anyone else her age."[4] Don'tcha love it?

I think of some of my "mentors" and take courage. At one hundred, Grandma Moses gave a birthday party for herself and danced a jig. May Sarton published her journal *At Seventy* when she was that age, claiming she was more complete and a richer person than at the age of twenty-five. Well, of course! At eighty-two, Henri Matisse completed his enormous five-year commission of designing and decorating the small chapel of Saint-Marie du Rosaire at Vence, France. I was in that chapel in 2000 and can tell you from experience it's one of the most beautiful buildings in the world.

Such color and symmetry! Such grace!

✼ ✼ ✼

*Lord, no matter how many days you give me on this earth, help me not take a single one for granted. Out of your* boundless grace, you have given me another day to live. And out of my deepest gratitude, I will "delight in every light-filled hour" of today, glorifying you in everything I do. Amen.

# 7

# An Unexpected Companion

~ Carol Kent ~

For the Scriptures say, "He will order his angels to protect and guard you."

—Luke 4:10 NLT

The invitation came unexpectedly. I first met Rebecca, a staff member for an international campus ministry organization, when she attended a mandatory communications training seminar I was conducting. She clearly wasn't happy about being there. She avoided eye contact, and her arms were crossed in a way that communicated her displeasure with being forced to attend a structured class on how to make effective presentations.

I didn't need a degree in psychology to read her thoughts: *I dare you to turn me into a cookie-cutter version of your definition of a good speaker!* It took a few hours for Rebecca to realize the training was not intended to force her to fit into a predetermined mold of an effective communicator. By the end of the three-day "Speak Up With Confidence" seminar, I was impressed with Rebecca's gut-level authenticity and zeal for ministry.

Now, fifteen years later, Rebecca is in international leadership with the same organization, and her main focus is to train women to take the gospel to strategic areas of the globe where the truth has not been heard. In an e-mail to me, she warmly recalled her initial resistance at the time of our first meeting. She wrote, "I remember how much I didn't want to be told how to speak—but instead of making me conform to a stereotypical speaker, you allowed me to be myself and to communicate within the framework of my own personality. Carol, would you consider coming to China to train about one hundred female campus leaders who primarily work in countries that are closed to the gospel?" She added, "The attendees are hungry to learn." I agreed to bring a team to train her leaders.

While making preparations for this trip, I had to comply with the rules, limits, and boundaries of going to a Communist country. Our team not only needed passports, but we also had to obtain special visas to be permitted to enter the country. My training materials had to be translated into Chinese and Korean. I learned there would be headset translation so participants would hear my teaching in their native tongues. My diction needed to be clear so the translators wouldn't miss anything. For a trip of this importance, we needed boundless prayer—for safety, for effectiveness in ministry, for good health, for speedy recovery from jetlag, for the Holy Spirit to translate the meaning behind the words to every woman—no matter what language she spoke.

We arrived at the Beijing airport on time, and we were immediately transported to our hotel. As we entered the lobby, there was great commotion. There were several American couples meeting their soon-to-be-adopted children for the first time. The excitement in the room was electric, and I felt privileged to witness such a glorious moment in the lives of children being lovingly embraced by their new parents. There were tears of joy splashing boundless love to all corners of the expansive atrium.

After a few hours of much-needed sleep, we met the local team leaders for breakfast and set up for the training. Later that day, the participants arrived—103 strong. Some women had traveled great distances to attend this multiple-day event. Their anticipation was palpable. Most of the attendees of were in their early to midtwenties, recent university graduates who were actively involved in ministry, especially evangelism. They needed to develop the necessary speaking skills to make topical presentations on recognizable needs and to learn how to weave the gospel into their talks in an understandable way. I have rarely spoken to a more enthusiastic group. Their passion for God and love for people motivated them to want to do their best.

Two days into this trip, I met a remarkable woman named

Elizabeth. She was one of the oldest participants, now in her thirties, and she was a mentor to many of these dedicated young women. I learned she had been one of the first women to teach English as a second language in one of the countries represented in our group, so I asked her to tell me about her pioneer work in cross-cultural evangelism.

"Soon after I arrived in the country, several young women came to Christ," she said, her face radiating with immense joy. "They were hungry to know more about God, and they longed for instruction in biblical principles."

I asked, "Did you have any moments of uncertainty or times that were particularly challenging, times when you questioned whether or not God's protection was surrounding your ministry?"

"Oh, yes," she answered truthfully. "I made multiple trips out of the country to raise support and to visit my family, and each time I returned I brought Bibles and study materials back with me. On one of my return trips, I was caught with this contraband at the border, and I was not allowed to return to the women I was mentoring."

"That must have been so disappointing," I said. "Did you ever see them again?"

"Well," Elizabeth continued, "two years passed, and I longed to see how these new Christians were growing in their faith. By this time I had learned of one border-crossing point where the customs inspection was less comprehensive, so I tried to enter the country there." Several women in our seminar were now crowded around our table to hear what happened next.

Elizabeth paused, choking back emotion, and said, "But when the customs officer fed my passport ID number into their electronic equipment, they discovered I had been banished from the country and I was immediately arrested."

For the next four days, Elizabeth was in a cement block room, with only one tiny window to the outside world. She recounted her surprise when one of the female guards entered her cell and commanded, "Sing me song, in English."

Elizabeth sang softly, "Jesus loves me, this I know, for the Bible tells me so."

"Sing me song—again!" the guard demanded. After she had sung the song at least nine times, one of the male guards entered Elizabeth's cell.

With pride, the female guard spoke up: "Listen, I learn song in English." With great delight, the female guard sang to her coworker, "Jesus loves me, this I know, for the Bible tells me so." Both guards eventually left the cell, proud that they had learned a bit of English.

Elizabeth gazed at the window overlooking the nation she loved, and she began to pray for the guards and for God to touch this expansive country with his truth. "Within a short time," she said, "I realized God had a different purpose than I did for this trip. He wanted me to use my cell as a place of prayer—so I began to outline the borders of the country in my mind and asked God to touch these people with his boundless love and draw them to himself."

At the end of the fourth day, Elizabeth was released to return to her own home. One of the guards drove her to the border, where she would again be free. During the trip, in broken English, he asked, "Who was that man who was with you the night we first arrested you?"

"No one was with me," Elizabeth responded. "I was alone."

"No!" the guard stated vehemently. "Who was that man who was with you, the man who refused to leave your side, no matter what?"

At that moment, Elizabeth realized that God had sent an angel, invisible to her but visible to her captors, to be her protector. God had a different plan for her ministry than she did on this trip. This country had put restrictions on what could be taught about Christ and the Bible, but God was not bound by those man-made limitations. Elizabeth discovered God's boundless grace when he transformed her cell into a prayer chamber.

The next time you face seemingly insurmountable obstacles, limitations, and man-made barriers, stop and look for the window of hope that will give you the vision to begin praying effectively for the people around you. You will experience genuine peace as your heart is quiet and at rest in His presence.

✼ ✼ ✼

*Father, I am so quick to assume you have vacated my personal space when life doesn't go according to my plan. Help me to understand that when you seem the most absent, you are boundlessly present—working all situations together for my good and for your glory.*

# 8

# Grace and Character Building

~ Marilyn Meberg ~

May you always be filled with the fruit of your salvation—
the righteous character produced in your life by Jesus
Christ—for this will bring much glory and praise to God.
—Philippians 1:11 NLT

Did you hear about the twelve-foot pet Burmese python that swallowed an entire queen-size electric blanket as well as the electrical cord and control box? According to the snake owner, the blanket was used to keep the reptile warm, but it somehow got mixed in with dinner. A fearless and competent veterinarian conducted a two-hour operation on the python and removed the blanket, cord, and control box. Her prognosis for the python's recovery is great.[5]

Since I am often prone to make parables of what I read and hear, the thought occurred to me that we, like the python, don't always know what's good for us. It's the not knowing that can work against our well-being and best interests.

Many of us miss knowing what's good for us and often don't even think about the consequences of not knowing. One of the major "knowings" parents must have is how crucial it is to release our young adult children into the mainstream of life. If we don't "let them go," the consequence is dependent and underdeveloped kids who never learn they can make it on their own without the parental safety net. They may swallow a blanket or two along the way, but they need to learn for themselves what's best for them.

When I left home at the age of eighteen to go to Seattle Pacific University, I was scared and exhilarated as I walked onto that campus. I was scared because I knew I would not have daily access to my parents and exhilarated because I was entering life on my own. Navigating that mainstream of life included some very tender moments of grace that I experienced from my parents, as well as new understandings of God's grace as he patiently taught me the value of personal discipline.

Dorm life was exceedingly appealing because, as an only child, I was not used to living around "sisters" who were almost always available for fun. One of the girls had a car, which added to our fun. Our favorite outing was to a nineteen-cent hamburger place called Dags. We'd pile into Darlene's car and joyously supplement our food intake with a burger, an order of fries, and a milkshake. We'd get back seconds before the dorm curfew of ten o'clock.

Not many weeks into the first semester, I realized physics class could ruin my academic scholarship. When I got a D on my first test, I was horrified as well as terrified. I called home for support from my parents. They were warmly sympathetic, but there was nothing they could do to pull me through physics. I knew they could not change my circumstances, but with that knowing came the deep-down understanding that, humanly speaking, I was truly on my own.

My father said, "You have a great opportunity to prove yourself to yourself: are you doing all you can to accomplish that?" Visions of my Dags hamburger run the night before the first physics test flashed before me. My rationalization had been, "This stuff does not make sense to me anyway," so I had grabbed my Dags money and crawled into Darlene's crowded car. "No point in studying something no college freshman should have to try to figure out," I said to my buddies. They all agreed and off we went. I was on the verge of a blanket swallow.

My father's question echoed in my head for several days. I realized I was not doing everything I could to prove myself to myself. As I think back on my father's response to my physics dilemma, I'm impressed by his wisdom. Because I was on an academic scholarship, the only way my parents could afford to send me to SPU was on the scholarship. But he did not remind me my future at SPU depended upon my performance. He knew I knew that. Neither did he suggest I make fewer Dags hamburger runs. He knew I was coming to know that. Instead, he appealed to my sense of self: "Are you doing everything you can to prove yourself to yourself?"

I was well aware that my father's financially impoverished background pushed him to prove himself to himself. His example of self-determination and self-reliance was a great model for me. But I had to choose for myself; I doubled my study time for physics and also got a tutor. She was a brilliant girl living on my dorm floor who rarely joined in our social activities; she was always studying. We were in the same physics class, so she began patiently explaining the unexplainable until I began to sorta get it. I managed ultimately to get a C in the class. That C was embarrassing to me, but at least I did not lose my scholarship. My A in psychology balanced out my semester grade point. My tutor and I celebrated our victory with double burgers at Dags; I paid.

I learned a lot about the parental safety net as I continued my youthful swim in the mainstream of life. I realized my parents were warm, loving, and available to the needs of my soul. But whether or not I should marry Ken Meberg, move to California, sign the teaching contract with Garden Grove School District, or buy a TV set were decisions I had to make for myself. Letting me go meant letting me decide. In that deciding, I might come dangerously close to swallowing a blanket or two, but sometimes that danger taught me far more than the protection from a bad decision.

Let me hasten to say that releasing our adult children does not mean we refuse to share our opinions or even give advice when asked. But if our opinions or advice are given to control a child's decision rather than facilitate that decision, we are encouraging our child's dependence upon us. That continued dependence contributes to an underdeveloped psyche prone to panic and uncertainty.

I think the experience of allowing God's grace to meet us in our need can be likened to the parent who stands back and lets a child choose to soar or fall. In a life full of queen-size blankets, we learn more from our falls than from our victories. God, ever the good parent, allows us a wide playing field to experience both.

Each of us is entrusted with certain capabilities and specific gifts that God means for us to develop. That usually requires discipline from us. Our development is not automatic or effortless. God's grace entrusts to us what he could develop for us, but he instead leaves the development to us. He is not indifferent or detached, but he grants us the dignity of living up to our God-given potentialities.

I well remember my "God, help me!" prayers about physics, but I also remember the sure knowledge I needed to put feet to my prayers. That meant I had to skip some Dags hamburger runs, find a tutor, and knuckle down and study. Not even God would do that for me; it was my job. He was there with me, though; he has promised that he will never leave me. However, his promise is not that he'd do everything instead of me. God knows that to do it all for me would work against my best interests.

What is in my best interest? God seems to think the building of my character—my endurance to persevere—is in my interest. James 1:3–4 says, "For you know that when your faith is tested, your endurance has a chance to grow. So let it grow, for when your endurance is fully developed, you will be perfect and complete, needing nothing" (NLT).

I don't think James had my ability to endure physics in mind when he wrote that basic spiritual promise, but I think that premise applies to everything we find humanly challenging. Our challenges are opportunities for us to develop spiritual muscles as well as character muscles. In it all is God's grace, available to us and always dispensed with God's fatherly wisdom.

✻ ✻ ✻

*Heavenly Father, like a good parent, you are helping me develop my spiritual muscles and character muscles. Today, help me see any challenges I encounter as glimpses of your grace—opportunities for me to strengthen my character and to become a little more like Christ. Amen.*

# 9

# All-Star Grace

~ Sandi Patty ~

My grace is sufficient for you, for my power is made perfect in weakness.
—2 Corinthians 12:9 NIV

We have been spending our summer at the baseball field. In fact, we spent the past few summers at the baseball field. Our son Sam loves baseball—and I have to say, he can really hit that ball. He is playing now in what is called the "major" league for ten- to eleven-year-olds. But like most kids, Sam started off playing coaches pitch T-ball for two summers, and we had a ball cheering with the other parents and grandparents at the games. It is a hoot to watch some of the really young ones run the wrong way on the bases or decide that the outfield is as good a place as any to go to the bathroom so they just "drop 'em." I finally took my video camera and got some great moments from a couple of games.

When Sam was about five, he played catcher and was doing okay, but he wasn't being aggressive enough to tag a guy out when he came from third base to home. I remember telling Sam that if he tagged a guy out at home, I would run out onto the field and pick him up and twirl him around right there at home plate. I'm not sure either of us thought I would actually do it.

Well, wouldn't you know, toward the end of the very next game, a runner came from third and was heading home. One of the other kids threw the ball to Sam at home plate—and Sam caught and tagged the guy out. Then he looked up at me and grinned under his catcher's mask as if to ask, *Well . . . are you gonna do it?* So I did. I ran onto the field—you know the dads were just dying—and I picked up Sam and twirled him around. We both just giggled. He did tell me on the way home from the game, "Mom, now you know when I get to the pros, you won't be able to do that." Duh!

One of the biggest honors for these young boys is to be chosen for the All-Star team at the end of the season. This consists of three or four players from each of the twelve teams, and they play tournaments for another month. Last year Sam didn't make it because it was his first year, and honestly he was just learning the game. However, this year he has worked hard and has been consistently one of the better players on his team. We had already picked out in our minds who the four players from our team would be: Chandler and Levi—Sam's two very best friends. And then another kid, Jacob. We had Sam picked for the fourth. I don't know who was more into our armchair team selection—Sam or us. (We didn't talk about it a whole lot in front of Sam "just in case.") But anyway, Don and I thought we had it all figured out. Sam even talked about how fun it would be to play on All-Stars with Chandler and Levi.

We had a big team party after our final game of the season, and Don and I overheard other parents talking about how they needed to take their kid to the All-Star tryouts that same evening. As we began to inquire, our hearts sank. We checked and rechecked our voice mail on our house phone and both of our cell phones. No message. Sam had not been called, and he had not been asked to be an All-Star.

Later, we found out that they had chosen only three players from our team, not four. We knew we had to tell Sam, but we didn't want it to be too big of a deal or too little of a deal, you know what I mean? Finally, Sam heard Chandler say something about All-Stars and asked us if anyone had called him. We shared with him that we hadn't gotten a call and that he wouldn't be in All-Stars. Don and I were trying so hard not to cry in front of him. He had really worked hard and had improved so much. The sweetest thing was to see how Chandler reacted. He was so disappointed that Sam wasn't going to be playing with them.

Well, we let the news settle with Sam. He was kind of quiet for a little while and then he got right back to being his energetic and wild self. Still, Don and I, and now Papa (my dad) were having a difficult time with it. After a couple of hours, my dad just couldn't stand it anymore. He got one of his old trophies (and he has many, many trophies from his years of sports) and took the nameplate off. He then brought it to our house to give to Sam. He told Sam that he wanted him to have this trophy because he felt Sam had been the Most Valuable Player on his team. What a picture of grace— our son received a trophy he did not earn but was freely given by his loving grandfather.

By this point, Don and I were crying and Papa was crying and Sam's eyes were as big as saucers. Sam took the trophy and held it and looked at it and then hugged it. It was an amazing moment. My dad, who truly has been Mr. Athlete all of his life, said that when he was Sam's age he never made an All-Star team, but he was given the trophy for Most Valuable Player.

Okay, so we didn't exactly play by the rules of the summer baseball league, but we played by the rule at the moment that said Sam needed a little nudge of encouragement. It may not have been the way everyone else did it, but for Sam, it was what was meant to be, and it meant a great deal to all of us. Sam was still a little disappointed that he wouldn't be playing All-Stars with his friends, but in the midst of that, there was a blessing that meant even more.

This was an eternal moment—it reminded me of how God takes our hurts and gives us back something better.

Sometimes our rules don't look exactly like God's, but then he's been playing the game a lot longer than we have. God doesn't take our hurt away, but he shares it alongside us, helping us to learn and grow from it. And he gives us a blessing in the midst of it. I'll play on his team, any day!

✳ ✳ ✳

*Lord, during those times when your rules aren't what I would have chosen, I will trust you anyway because you always do what is best for me. By your boundless grace, you are helping me learn and grow, and I am blessed. Amen.*

# 10

# Make Space for Grace

~ Patsy Clairmont ~

But when Daniel learned that the law had been signed, he
went home and knelt down as usual in his upstairs room,
with its windows open toward Jerusalem. He prayed three
times a day, just as he had always done, giving thanks to
his God.

—Daniel 6:10 NLT

Space matters.

For instance, when we bought our home six years ago, I
thought the closet in our bedroom was humungous. I was
certain the military could use it as a hangar for their aircraft
or U-Haul could park a fleet of trucks in it. Truth is, though,
not only couldn't I wedge my baby PT Cruiser into my closet,
but also now I can't find an available slot for a hankie. Somebody shrunk my closet?

Of course before I moved to this home, my closet was
the size of a mailbox. Once I crammed a garment in it, I didn't
know if I'd ever find it again or if it would be pressed into

oblivion. So when I moved into this house where one could actually step into the closet and turn around, the comparison left me thinking I had boundless room. But life has a way of expanding . . . as does our girth, which adds to my growing wardrobe dilemma. The sizes in my closet are as varied as ice cream flavors at Cold Stone, which probably gives you a clue as to the pudgy portion of my attire.

Speaking of pudgy, I bought a plump new chair for my living room the other day because I had a vacant space left when I "loaned" two chairs to my children for their store. I carefully examined many furniture offerings on the market before I made my chair decision. My husband and I brought it home and, guess what, it didn't work—the color tone was off. And because it was on sale it wasn't returnable. Oh, great. So I began to hunt around my house to determine where I might use it. We hauled it to my office, and then we took the office chair and put it in the living room. But the new chair was too paunchy for the space, so we moved it to the bedroom. To fit it in there we had to remove a table, which we relocated in the living room. To get the table in, I had to move a small cabinet, which visited several spaces before ending up in my bedroom. Now my bedroom was ready to explode with all the additional pieces, so I had to sacrifice a dresser and two lamps, which went home with my son.

I had seemingly settled the new purchase into its cubby, but now I had no chair in my office. Off we boogied to the basement, where I commandeered a rocker that I put in the hearth room and swiped the hearth chair for the empty office space. I must confess the former hearth chair looked odd since it was covered in roosters, so I swiped a throw from a bedroom and tried to disguise the print. Oh, and did I mention that the chair was dwarfed by my office set and high ceilings, which made it look like Tinkerbell furniture? To help hide the last of the roosters on the fabric, I tossed a pillow on it. And as if to add to the confusion of the viewer, the pillow is emblazoned with these words: "Big Girl."

Space matters.

Whether we are positioning a chair or prioritizing our prayer life, space matters. A friend called me yesterday and confessed that life keeps crowding out her prayer time. She said her intentions are good, and then slowly the space she had designated for talking to the Lord is used up by unanticipated demands.

I totally understood. Just as I couldn't have imagined when I purchased a chair what hubbub it would cause or time it would take to just find a place for it, I often am surprised how life eats up my purposed goals. The alarm doesn't go off, the phone rings again, a child throws up, unexpected guests arrive, the dog needs to be rushed to the vet, yada, yada, yada. Life is invasive.

It reminds me of that old video game Ms. Pac-Man, where round smiley-faced fellows ate up dots in an attempt to devour "you" and put you out of the game, while you ran lickety-split through a maze.

I thought of Old Testament Daniel and how he prayed three times a day without fail. And even when smiley-faced fellows outlawed the bending of one's knee to anyone except the king in hopes of wiping Daniel out, he continued his vigilant prayer routine.

Imagine being banished into a den of lions as their appetizer, and your only crime was talking to the Lord. I'll tell you what, had that been me, I know my prayer life would have deepened quickly. A single growl from yonder surly beast, and I would have no more excuses, no more procrastination, and no more diversions. No siree, just unadulterated, passionate, "I got time for you, Lord" prayer.

There is something about crisis that helps us pray with fervor and also to reprioritize. Have you noticed that?

Perhaps, if we designated a space and time for prayer, that would help dedicate us to those important moments between God and us. Then what if we turned off our phones or let them go to voice mail? What if we kindly let our friends and kin know we were not available from seven till eight o'clock in the morning? Or nine to ten o'clock at night? And what if we asked our struggling prayer friend to gently hold us accountable and we would return the favor. Hmm, might work. Could be worth a try. Whatcha think?

Scripture tells us that Daniel was a man who had "an

excellent spirit" in him (Daniel 6:3 NKJV). Daniel had already passed the necessary criteria to be considered for his palace position: handsome, gifted in all wisdom, possessing knowledge, quick to understand, and a servant with a teachable heart. Whoa, those are tough qualifications. Yet Daniel more than aced the course on integrity personified—and get this, he was only a teenager when he was taken into captivity. How impressive is that? Why he seems almost boundless in character.

Here's my question: do you think Daniel just had good DNA, a strong upbringing, or do you think his prayer life cultivated his character? The phrase that caught my attention in Daniel 6:10 is at the end of the verse: "as was his custom since early days."

"As was his custom" was referring to Daniel's regular prayer life. Sounds like being a man of prayer was a way of life for him.

Now what about for us? Let's establish a plan. I've decided that I will perch on my rooster chair in the morning (cock-a-doodle-do) to talk with the Lord about my day and then rollerblade (okay, okay, toddle) to the chubby chair in the cubby for my evening prayers. I've placed Bibles by both chairs with notepads and pens. Now what space will you set apart for him?

Next, I made a prayer list because I count heavily on paper to fill in the discrepancies of my brain cells. (I am not Daniel.)

Sometimes I hold pictures of those I'm praying for because it seems to add another level of personalization. Who is on your list?

Sometimes my list is so long I have to do half in the morning and half in the evening. And I've learned when life disrupts my prayers, which it will from time to time, not to be discouraged but simply to begin again as soon as circumstances allow. Some things are outside our control. We don't want to be so married to our schedule that we lose our flexibility, and yet we don't want to disregard this time for every passing whim.

I personally find it helpful to read a daily devotional reading before I pray to pull in my stray thoughts. Sometimes I just begin with a psalm.

The most important step in prayer is to begin. Don't worry about how you say what's on your mind because, while we are speaking, God is reading our hearts. He hears even the deep stuff we don't know how to articulate. And he filters all our inner chaos through his boundless grace. God gets us.

So find your space, even if it's a small barnyard chair in a tall room, and I promise you once you begin this prayer pattern you will walk through the day feeling like a "Big Girl."

✻ ✻ ✻

*God, I will find a space to meet with you every day—starting today! I want to be a woman of character, for whom prayer is a way of life. Thank you for meeting me in my prayer space and reaching out to fill my heart with your boundless grace. Amen.*

# UNFATHOMABLE
# GRACE

# 11

# Dad's Final Flight

~ Carol Kent ~

The faithful love of the LORD never ends! His mercies never cease.

—Lamentations 3:22 NLT

My husband smiled as he put down the phone. "Guess who's coming for a visit!" I wasn't sure who he was talking about because, since moving to Florida a year and a half earlier, we had enjoyed numerous visits from family members and friends. By now Gene was grinning from ear to ear. "My dad wants to drive down from Michigan, and he's bringing my brother Monty with him."

Monty was diagnosed with lung cancer at age forty-seven, and we knew his prognosis was not good. Neither of them had been able to visit our son since his incarceration seven and a half years earlier, and they were eager to see him. At age eighty-two, with diabetes and multiple health challenges, we were surprised Gene's dad felt well enough to make the trip.

A couple of days passed, and Gene and I discussed the visit. "Let's check to see if there are any mileage tickets available," I quipped. "Wouldn't it be great fun and much easier on both of them physically if they could fly here in a few hours instead of an exhausting two-day drive?" I was getting excited about helping to plan this adventure for my father-in-law and my brother-in-law. Sure enough, the tickets were available.

Dad and Monty flew to Tampa on a direct flight on a picture-perfect day. Their excitement about the flight was unforgettable. Monty piped up, "This is the first time either of us has flown since we were in the army. It was so much fun to see the earth from a bird's-eye view!"

The next two weeks were filled with fun activities, including the Webster Flea Market, with one square mile of sales stalls featuring every imaginable array of garage-sale items at drastically discounted prices. Dad and Monty carefully selected items they knew their family members would enjoy as gifts. Then came the trip to Plant City's Strawberry Festival, where we gorged ourselves on the biggest strawberry shortcakes on the menu—complete with ice cream and whipped cream. Dad was living in the moment, engaging the children around him in conversation and loving every minute of the afternoon. In retrospect, I think he was aware that his days were numbered and life was not to be wasted or taken lightly.

We had sit-down family dinners every night, and Dad enjoyed the laughter and banter around the table, lingering to capture every minute of time with two of his sons. Dad had been a Grand Trunk Railroad plumber in Durand, Michigan, during the days when more than one hundred trains a day passed through his little hometown. He shared some of his memories, and then my husband chimed in, recounting the story of the day he disobeyed his father.

There was a house rule during Gene's growing-up years. His family lived in a home near the railroad tracks and often there were boxcars parked there, waiting for an engine to take them to their next destination. Gene imitated his Dad's voice as he recounted a familiar warning from much earlier years: "Don't *ever* climb the boxcars! In fact, I never want you boys to go *near* the boxcars!"

To his sons, that rule seemed ridiculous. Young neighborhood boys regularly climbed the boxcars. They made a game out of climbing up the eighteen-foot-high ladder and then running at top speed across the top of the fifty-foot-long car and getting the momentum to jump to the next car, and the next, and the next. There were sometimes as many as fifteen to twenty boxcars waiting on the tracks, and the sport of running, combined with the danger of falling, made this activity very popular to the unsupervised ten- to twelve-year-old-boys who regularly engaged in it.

Gene's mother worked at a local battery plant eight hours a day, and the babysitter was often distracted. One afternoon Gene gazed with envy at the boys who were laughing and running with gusto on the nearby boxcars. He rationalized that the babysitter would never know, and his parents were both at work, so he would not get caught if he joined his friends this one time. Racing to the railroad tracks, he grabbed the ladder and quickly made his way to the top of the first boxcar. From this vantage point he had an excellent view of the nearby street. He instantly spotted his father's truck—and their eyes locked in a way that only a parent and a disobedient child understand.

Instantly, Gene scrambled down the steps and raced for the house. When he got home, his dad's truck was already in the driveway. Dad emerged, taking off his belt as he ran to his son. Gene's words tumbled out: "I won't ever climb the boxcars again! I won't sass Mom! I'll be good—I promise!" But it was too late. Gene was disciplined, and he never forgot the boxcar rule again. His father's action seemed harsh at the moment, but he was unrelenting for good reason. Dad had been around long enough to see coworkers lose arms or legs, or even their lives, when there were accidents on the tracks. He loved his sons too much to take unnecessary chances.

Years later, Gene realized the immeasurable love that prompted his father's disciplinary action. After having a son of our own, we finally understood that kind of love. It's the same kind of love God has for each of us—loving us enough to chastise us when we get off track, caring for us deeply when we are about to fall. Loving us so much he sent his son to die on the cross to pay the price for our wrongdoings. That act is so unthinkable we have trouble understanding it—but because of God's infinite grace toward us, we are the recipients of love beyond measure.

The dictionary says *unfathomable* means "not capable of being fathomed: immeasurable, impossible to comprehend." That's a perfect description of the love of our Father God. It's the kind of love most parents have for their children—it simply defies description. There is nothing we wouldn't do to save our children from getting hurt or from making devastating choices.

During his two-week visit in our home, Dad visited the Christian bookstore and picked up a couple of sing-along DVDs of great songs of the faith. I found myself cringing when he turned the volume up to my discomfort level in order to compensate for his loss of hearing. Moments later, I heard a sweeter sound. It was Dad singing along with the video in the most charming monotone I've ever heard. He was singing about heaven with his eyes closed and a smile curving up the corners of his mouth. I knew he was thinking about unfathomable glory in a place he was headed for soon. In that moment, the volume no longer mattered and his monotone became a cherished sound.

The visit ended all too quickly, and Dad and Monty made the trip home. Seven weeks later, we received a call: "Mom checked on Dad at seven a.m., and he was sleeping peacefully.

A little after eight o'clock, he just quit breathing and woke up in heaven."

Because of God's unfathomable love for us, his children, we who believe in him will one day wake up in a place that defies description—heaven.

In the meantime, we may sometimes question his love when it seems he reprimands us when we run headway in the wrong direction. And then, usually much later, we realize when we finally quit running, we can't resist his love. It's unfathomable, unchanging, immeasurable—impossible to comprehend.

✼ ✼ ✼

*Father, there are times when I don't feel your love, and I question your judgment. That usually happens when I'm running away from your principles and doubting your goodness. Help me to fully embrace your unfathomable love as I lean into the comfort of your arms. Amen.*

# 12

# Glimpses of Grace

~ Marilyn Meberg ~

And we believers also groan, even though we have the
Holy Spirit within us as a foretaste of future glory, for we
long for our bodies to be released from sin and suffering.
We, too, wait with eager hope for the day when God will
give us our full rights as his adopted children.

—Romans 8:23 NLT

At a time when the "bad side" of people is evident all
around us, I love experiencing the "good side." I love seeing people together in a show of caring camaraderie; it lifts
my spirits and comforts my heart. So I want to talk about
the girls at a department store makeup counter in Hartford,
Connecticut. I'll tell you what led me to them.

On August 10, 2006, I was picked up at 7:30 a.m. for the
"airport run." The Women of Faith speakers were heading for
Hartford, Connecticut, for our conference there. I had heard
only a snatch of news about the terrorist plot to down ten
American airplanes that necessitated last-minute heightened

security for all air travel. My friend and traveling companion Pat Wenger called and warned me to not pack any liquids in my carry-on luggage. I hastily ditched my bottle of water, grabbed my roller bag, and headed for the door.

After an hour's wait in the security line, I was stunned and horrified as I helplessly watched two airport security men methodically toss out every tube and bottle of makeup I owned into a refuse bin. When they took my cleansing creams and other wrinkle camouflaging cover-ups and nonchalantly dropped them into the bin, my heart sank. *Do they have any idea how much it costs to keep me from looking ninety-five?*

But the worst was yet to come. My bottle of Calandre perfume, which I had pounced upon for purchase when we were in Calgary, Canada, a week ago, was also dropped unceremoniously into the bin. I've been wearing that perfume for at least eighty-four years, and it's hard to find. Except to the very ancient, the perfume is a forgotten scent. I can get it off the Internet, and though the effort is rewarding, it is indeed an effort. So to find this big bottle of Calandre in Calgary was a weekend highlight.

Within the hour we were informed that our flight to Chicago with a connection to Hartford had been cancelled. A sympathetic agent rerouted us on a direct flight. "Gotcha booked . . . so run to the next terminal and you should make it."

"What about our checked bags?" I asked.

"Don't know, honey. Just run!"

We arrived in Hartford; our bags did not. They were loitering around somewhere in Chicago with no guarantee of catching up with us. Pat and I took off to buy pajamas, face putty, and—maybe—perfume.

As I told my tale of cosmetic woe to the girls at the various counters, they gathered around me with horror and empathy. Then they scurried off to their product line tables and returned with packets and packets of samples. One of them asked what perfume I liked. She had heard of Calandre, but of course no one carried it. Several of them started filling little vials with various perfumes they thought I'd like. With a collective sigh of relief and accomplishment, they sent me out of the store and on to face the world.

Those in the Hartford audience may have noticed I had a certain glow all weekend. Part of the glow was due to my new foundation makeup; it was a bit darker than I usually wear. But my glow sprang primarily from the images of my dear sisters from the cosmetics counter who demonstrated such kindness to me in my time of need.

When we experience the kindness of others, it makes us feel we live in a safe world, populated by safe people who have our best interests at heart. I well remember Mr. Delbert, who lived in our small community in Washington State. Mr. Delbert fascinated my eight-year-old mind because he was a nonstop smoker, smelled bad, didn't go to church, but smiled a lot. He had nine cats, three dogs, and other "comin' and goin'" creatures that roamed his small property. He frequently sat on a bench outside Boehm's grocery store and drank Pepsi Cola from a bottle.

I occasionally shared the bench with him, and together we'd drink Pepsi Cola from our respective bottles. That periodic shared sociability is how I happened to know he didn't give a fig about God and that he smelled bad. But Mr. Delbert had a huge, caring heart in spite of not giving a fig about God. It was Mr. Delbert who came running to help the Schwartz's cat when it got stuck at the top of their maple tree. It was Mr. Delbert who helped my dad install a new water heater in our house when the old one "gave out." It was also Mr. Delbert who blew up fifty balloons (no machine, just lungs) for our annual church bazaar. Mr. Delbert could be counted on to do good things for people.

One afternoon, I asked him why he never came to church. The community was small, so it was obvious who came and who didn't. He told me he didn't need church because he lived by the Golden Rule. That, he said, was all the church he needed. I wondered about that and asked my parents if they thought Mr. Delbert was a Christian. My dad said he didn't know. He told me Mr. Delbert was a great neighbor, but whether he was a Christian wasn't based on being a good neighbor; it was based on whether he knew Jesus as his Savior.

Several days later, I took up my position on the bench next to Mr. Delbert. I asked him if Jesus was his Savior. "Yup," he said. That was good enough for me; Mr. Delbert made the world a safer place whether he came to church or not. I didn't try to figure out how not going to church fit with knowing Jesus. That was beyond my grasp. But I know Mrs. Wentworth never missed a day of church, and I also knew she would never have helped rescue the cat at the top of Schwartz's tree.

When we experience loving-kindnesses, we are tapping into the world as it was meant to be. Kindness soothes our souls and comforts our heart. Everything in us rises up in opposition to the presence of evil; it feels so foreign . . . it does not belong here. The reality is, God did not create us to live in a world where the presence of evil must be accommodated. We were created for perfection. We lost the experience of Eden, but we still carry the stamp of divine expectation in our collective hearts. The reason I am comforted by kindness and goodness is because I was created for those experiences. And those moments when I experience kindness and goodness, I have a glimpse of not only what should have been but what is yet to come.

We all have a yearning for what is yet to come. Romans 8:25 says, "But if we look forward to something we don't yet have, we must wait patiently and confidently" (NLT). Ecclesiastes 3:11 says that God has planted eternity in our hearts. That ancient heart-yearn has a divine root. There will come a time when we will live in a strife-free, kindness-infused environment. And when we do, we will remember we had glimpses of it before. Some of my glimpses include the cosmetics counter employees in Hartford and the eccentric goodness of Mr. Delbert.

These are glimpses of God's grace. Grace for me, grace from him, grace for us all.

✡ ✡ ✡

*Lord, I long for the future day when you will judge evil and restore the world to how it was meant to be. But for now, open my eyes to see the glimpses of your grace that you have placed all around me. Amen.*

# 13

# Out of Egypt

~ Luci Swindoll ~

By faith Moses, when he had grown up, refused to be
known as the son of Pharaoh's daughter. . . . He regarded
disgrace for the sake of Christ as of greater value than the
treasures of Egypt, because he was looking ahead to the
reward.

—Hebrews 11:24, 26 NIV

Since I was a little girl I've been intrigued by the country of
Egypt . . . that exotic seat of civilization. As an art major
in college, Egyptology fascinated me. I've always been curious about Egyptian ruins, mummies, temples, museums,
artifacts, and most especially, that long, life-giving thread that
cuts the country in half—the Nile River. Even the Sahara
Desert held a certain amount of intrigue.

For decades I read everything I could find on Egypt and
pondered its mysteries. The hieroglyphics, with all their for-
midable intricacies and intrigue, were like magnets, inviting
me to analyze what was written and why. It's been said this

language is the most difficult ever put into writing . . . beautiful to look at but almost impossible to read. It uses pictographs, which are highly stylized symbols, representing complex ideas. Nevertheless, I was curious about the messages they conveyed.

Egypt has been very careful to preserve its monuments and treasures, spending a fortune to protect them and see that they're treated with dignity and respect. And not only have Egyptians spent money on their preservation efforts, but so have other nations on behalf of Egypt. For example, in 1952 when the Egyptian government found it necessary to build a new dam just upstream from Aswan, various ancient archeological sites along the bank of the Nile were threatened. Lifting twelve of these monolithic treasures to higher ground proved to be prohibitively expensive, so other nations from around the world helped to bear that cost. It was a gigantic, worldwide team effort.

People are simply confounded when it comes to a study of Egypt. For more than three millennia, humanity has been marveling at Egypt's wonders. About 450 years before the birth of Christ, the Greek geographer Herodotus wrote in *The Histories*, "Nowhere are there so many marvelous things, nor in the whole world beside are there to be seen so many things of unspeakable greatness."

In December 2005, I had an opportunity to travel to Egypt and see firsthand what all these books had been talking about.

Suddenly, that vast land lay before me. I was mesmerized. I walked at the base of the pyramids . . . the same place where others had walked five thousand years before the birth of Christ. I floated up the Nile on a riverboat . . . the same river where Moses was hidden as a baby from the murderous designs of the Egyptian king. I went into tombs, some of which still held the remains of pharaohs and kings of that land. I saw statuaries and temples that represented centuries of architecture and design I had studied as a college student.

It was as though I went back into a time tunnel.

Into this ancient scene, Moses was born. Picture it in your mind. He was raised by the daughter of Pharaoh and lived as a child of great wealth. He was taught by Egyptian tutors in every imaginable field—science, medicine, philosophy, law, the arts, and hieroglyphics. Acts 7:22 tells us, "Moses was educated in all the wisdom of the Egyptians" (NIV). He likely attended school at the Temple of the Sun, which would be like Oxford today. Moses was intelligent, diligent, influential, bold, and courageous. The pride of Egypt, he was the next heir to the throne of Pharaoh. But note what Hebrews 11:24–27 says:

> By faith Moses, when he had grown up, refused to be known as the son of Pharaoh's daughter. He chose to be mistreated along with the people of God rather than to enjoy the pleasures of sin for a short time. He regarded

disgrace for the sake of Christ as of greater value than the treasures of Egypt, because he was looking ahead to his reward. By faith he left Egypt, not fearing the king's anger; he persevered because he saw him who is invisible. (NIV)

How could Moses do that? What was inside Moses that enabled him to see "him who is invisible"? Why did he prefer disgrace more than all those priceless treasures? What was the reward ahead to which he looked forward?

I believe the collective answer to all those questions is *infinite grace*. God put into the heart of Moses the realization that there was something much better ahead of him. He didn't know what it was, but by faith he trusted God to show him when the time came . . . and he wanted to be prepared.

In Acts 7:20–29, we learn that when Moses was about the age of forty, he could no longer sit back and tolerate the inhumane treatment happening to his fellow Jews, who were being beaten under the lash of their taskmasters. At this time, verse 23 tells us, "it entered his mind" to visit his fellow Israelites. Moses saw them. He went to their defense. He rescued them. And in verse 25, we discover that Moses "supposed that his brethren understood that God was granting them deliverance through him."

Moses had an infinite calling. Somehow, and in some unrevealed way, Moses understood he would be the deliverer of the nation of Israel, even though that had not been revealed to anyone else. Although he acted rashly when he murdered the Egyptian and then fled Egypt, he was convinced that God had called him to that extraordinary role of deliverer way back then—not just when he stood before the burning bush at the age of eighty (Acts 7:30). It took that additional forty years for Moses to learn God's way of doing things: It's "not by might nor by power, but by my Spirit" (Zechariah 4:6 NIV) that God's work gets done. In the hard places of Moses' life, God kept his word because of his amazing, unfathomable, infinite grace.

At every turn, Moses experienced God's grace. He was reared in royalty so that he received the necessary schooling in preparation for service. That's grace. He was humbled by suffering so that he learned to stop taking measures into his own hands. That's grace. He was empowered by God so that he recognized his leadership abilities came from an almighty source. That's grace.

In all things . . . *grace*.

Look at our own culture. The resemblance to the time of Moses is obvious. We're surrounded by everything money can buy, but when we get it, we want something different. We don't know what, but what we have doesn't satisfy. We feel a calling inside that's bigger than ourselves. It's an invisible force on the horizon, pulling us toward it. What is that? It's God. He calls us to a life of grace with him. And one of the beauties of the life he offers is that it's not by might nor by power that things get done. It's by trusting his Spirit to work through us.

I'm just five years shy of the age of Moses when he stood at the burning bush and heard the voice of God saying, "So get yourself ready; I'm sending you" (Acts 7:34 MSG). While I know I'm certainly not Moses and this is not ancient Egypt, God has made our hearts alike and he has a purpose for everyone who knows him. By his unfathomable grace, I'll continue on this path as life unfolds.

✻ ✻ ✻

*God, like Moses, you have put into my heart the realization that there is something much better ahead of me. By faith, I trust you to reveal to me your plan in your time. Help me be prepared to fulfill your calling. Amen.*

# 14

# Available Grace

## ~ Sandi Patty ~

Is there any encouragement from belonging to Christ? Any comfort from his love? Any fellowship together in the Spirit? Are your hearts tender and compassionate? Then make me truly happy by agreeing wholeheartedly with each other, loving one another, and working together with one mind and purpose. Don't be selfish; don't try to impress others. Be humble, thinking of others as better than yourselves. Don't look out only for your own interests, but take an interest in others, too.

—Philippians 2:1–4 NLT

On June 5, 2003, Ron and Carolyn Patty, my parents, celebrated their fiftieth wedding anniversary. Unbelievable! At age seventy, they are still healthy, and they ride their bikes for an hour every day. But the best part of their fifty years together is that they love (and *like*) each other more than ever. They still kiss big on the lips, they tell each other "I love you" every day—in fact, they always see who can say it first in the morning—they hold hands when they go to a movie, and they love their children and grandchildren and have wonderful relationships with all of them.

I am so blessed to be their daughter. My parents have taught me many things about love and life. The word that comes to mind when I think about them is *available*. They are always available to anyone who needs them, whether it is our son Sam wanting to catch spiders or me needing a couple of big handyman jobs around the house or getting a frosty for any of their grandkids who may be sick. I want to be that available to others, especially to my husband and children, as I move through this journey of life.

We had a huge celebration for my parents this year. It was amazing. My brother Mike and his family came from Arizona. Mike is an awesome chef and he did all of the food for our reception afterward. My brother Craig and his wife were here as well. My mom's best friend of forty-eight years, Carol Cutler, and her two daughters came from Oklahoma. We invited some of my mom's friends from Anderson and some of my dad's golfing buddies.

Mom and Dad renewed their vows at a sweet little chapel on the Anderson University Campus. It was so awesome. We all went to the chapel early, and a sixteen-passenger white limo picked up Mom and Dad and brought them to the church. They were so surprised—now, it wasn't a total surprise, but many of the details we left out. We just asked them to be ready and dressed up by four o'clock. Our pastor, Jim

Lyon, officiated the ceremony. He recounted their life's journey and how God led each of them to each other. My husband, Don, stood as my dad's best man, while Sam stood as the ring bearer. My two brothers walked my mom down the aisle (while her good friend Shirley played "Maria's Theme" from *The Sound of Music*). When Pastor Jim asked, "Who gives this woman to be married to this man?" our whole family responded, "We all do!"

My parents said something to each other and made us all cry. After my dad shared all the things about my mom he loved—he actually wrote down one hundred things, but only shared ten of them with us in the ceremony—he asked my brother Craig to sing a song he has always loved from the musical *Scrooge*, called "You."

Then it was my mom's turn to say something to my dad. She shared how much he had meant to her, and we all cried again. She then had my brother Mike sing a song from *The Music Man* called "Till There Was You." Wow!

Then my brother Mike shared from his heart about family and what it means to all of us. It was so precious.

Don and I sang "The Prayer," which is a beautiful duet but very difficult to sing when you are crying out of such thankfulness. Ours were definitely happy tears.

Our friend Rick Vale, who has written many songs for me, wrote a song in honor of my parents, about how we all pass our light onto everyone we meet. While he was singing that song, the family began to light candles on the altar. One candle was already lit to represent God, from whom all of our light comes. Then my parents lit their candle from God's candle, and then my brothers and me and our spouses. Then all of our kids. When we finished, there were eighteen candles glowing brightly. What a beautiful picture of God's love and the life he continues to give to all of us.

The best part of the wedding was at the very end. Of course my dad gave my mom a huge kiss. All the kids thought it was gross in a beautiful kind of way. Then the organist played, as the recessional, "Take Me out to the Ball Game." Let me explain. My dad has always been an amazing athlete. He pitched fast-pitch softball and won many world tournaments in his day. He was playing for a team the summer he got married, and they just happened to have a game the night of their wedding. Being a committed athlete (and with the support of my mother), my dad played a softball game after the wedding reception. He actually wore his uniform under his tuxedo! Incidentally, he pitched a perfect game, which means no one on the other team even reached first base. He says he was in a bit of a hurry. So, that's where "Take Me out to the Ball Game" comes in. As the organist played, we all sang along and laughed and hugged and cried with joy.

My parents' relationship continues to amaze me. They really do think of the other one before they think of themselves. There are days I honestly don't understand it, but they tell me that when you truly think of the other person first and your spouse in return thinks of you first, your needs really do get met. Huh! I think Jesus had a concept that went something like that. But why is it that I am so skeptical of it working? I sometimes think I have to be the first one to speak my needs because if I don't, no one will know.

To tell you the truth, I used to have a much harder time with that one. I used to allow people to walk all over me and never spoke my mind. Perhaps in my older age and my post-therapy years, I have let the pendulum swing too far the other way. I'm not really sure. But when I see my parents, I realize that even though I don't always understand this kind of unselfish love and grace, I believe it is true because I see it alive in them. And the unconditional grace my parents show to each other every day is a reflection of the unfathomable grace God shows to each of us.

✳ ✳ ✳

*Lord, thank you for your unconditional love and grace toward me. Help me to reflect and share with others your forgiving, unselfish, unfathomable grace. Amen.*

# 15

# Always Welcomed Home

## ~ Sheila Walsh ~

When he was still a long way off, his father saw him. His heart pounding, he ran out, embraced him, and kissed him. The son started his speech: "Father, I've sinned against God, I've sinned before you; I don't deserve to be called your son ever again."

But the father wasn't listening. . . . "My son is here—given up for dead and now alive! Given up for lost and now found!" And they began to have a wonderful time.

—Luke 15:21-22, 24 MSG

Of all the stories that are quoted to illustrate the unfathomable grace of God, the story of the prodigal son has to be right there at the top of the list. Most of us know the story well. A father has two sons, one shows great disrespect for his father by asking for his share of his father's estate while the father is still very much alive. The young man takes off to the equivalent of our Las Vegas and becomes the life of the party . . . until his money runs out. When he is living on the streets, he remembers how well his father's servants are treated compared to the squalor he is living in. So he decides to go back home and ask his dad for a job. His father has been waiting for him day in and day out, just watching the road to see if perhaps today his boy will come home. The boy's narcissistic behavior has done nothing to weaken his father's love for him. As the son is halfway though his "I am a terrible son" speech, he realizes that his dad is not listening; he is planning a welcome home party.

But there is another son. This older son has played it by the books. He has tremendous respect for his father's work ethic and every day tries to outdo it. I'm sure he was disgusted with his rebellious younger brother; after all, he was the one who stayed home and watched the impact his brother's selfishness had on his father. He tries to pick up the slack and works even harder so that his dad doesn't have to worry about the family business. Then at the end of a long, tiring day, as he makes his way back home, he can hear noise coming from the house. It sounds like the celebration they had a few weeks ago when his cousin got married, but there was nothing scheduled for tonight. Curious, he picks up the tempo in his walk. He sees one of the servants and asks him what on earth is going on. At first he is stunned, and then his shock turns to rage. How could his father do this? To welcome his deadbeat brother back is like telling him everything he did was okay. Nothing makes sense to him anymore.

That's the way the kingdom of God is. It takes every-thing we understand to be true and covers it in grace. Grace should be the thing that unites us, but more often than not it is the thing that divides us. We weigh people's actions and consequences on our own human scales of justice—yet in God's economy, those scales don't work. I think of the people behind bars who in the quiet of their cells cry out to God for mercy. Many are suspicious of these jailhouse conversions, but I believe that no matter what brings us to the foot of the cross, when we find ourselves there, grace is offered.

Take a man like Tex Watson. He was born just a few miles away from where I live in Dallas, Texas. As a young man with no strong roots or beliefs, Tex headed out to California looking for peace, love, and rock and roll. Instead he met up with Charles Manson and became part of the infamous Manson family. On August 9, 1969, he and other Manson family members broke into the home of Hollywood actress Sharon Tate and murdered Sharon and four others. Sharon was two weeks away from giving birth. Upon his arrest, Tex Watson was sentenced to death. In 1972, his death sentence was overturned, and he was sentenced to life in prison.

As a nation, we were pretty much done with Tex Watson and the other Manson killers, but God was not. Tex's mom and dad, both of whom have since died, were very devoted believers. They wrote to several evangelists and asked them to visit their son in prison. Through one of those visits, in

1975, Charles "Tex" Watson asked Christ into his life. In 1980 he founded Abounding Love Ministries to minister to prisoners and their families, and in 1983 he became an ordained minister. Today, more than thirty-five years later, he still sits in prison but he uses every day to reach out to others with the love, grace, and mercy of God. Through his writings and online he reaches out to those who have lost hope. He is a housing unit janitor in prison, and he walks the prison yard bringing the light of Christ to a very dark place. The Abounding Love Web site makes it very clear that he firmly rejects any kind of legalistic Christianity:

> He boldly rejects the perception of legalistic Christianity, where people are led to believe they can earn their salvation through their own good works. He lives every day reaching out to unbelievers with the grace of God and prays with believers to understand their awesome inheritance because of their union with Christ's death, burial and resurrection.[6]

God's grace knows no boundaries. It can flow through prison bars and over church pews. It covers those in cancer wards and school yards. It softens the hearts of the runaways and the throwaways and calls to those who refuse to join in the celebration too. It is love. God's grace is love-felt. It is the outstretched arms of God that catch us when we fall. If we tried to write about it for the rest of our lives, the world would run out of ink.

✡ ✡ ✡

*The love of God is greater far*
*Than tongue or pen can ever tell;*
*It goes beyond the highest star,*
*And reaches to the lowest hell;*
*The guilty pair, bowed down with care,*
*God gave His Son to win;*
*His erring child He reconciled,*
*And pardoned from his sin.*

*O love of God, how rich and pure!*
*How measureless and strong!*
*It shall forevermore endure*
*The saints' and angels' song.*

*When years of time shall pass away,*
*And earthly thrones and kingdoms fall,*
*When men, who here refuse to pray,*
*On rocks and hills and mountains call,*
*God's love so sure, shall still endure,*
*All measureless and strong;*
*Redeeming grace to Adam's race—*
*The saints' and angels' song.*

*Could we with ink the ocean fill,*
*And were the skies of parchment made,*
*Were every stalk on earth a quill,*
*And every man a scribe by trade,*
*To write the love of God above,*
*Would drain the ocean dry.*
*Nor could the scroll contain the whole,*
*Though stretched from sky to sky.*

—Frederick M. Lehman

# 16

# Words of Grace

~ Pasty Clairmont ~

All Scripture is inspired by God and is useful to teach us what is true and to make us realize what is wrong in our lives. It corrects us when we are wrong and teaches us to do what is right. God uses it to prepare and equip his people to do every good work.

—2 Timothy 3:16–17 NLT

Unfathomable is all about immeasurable depth and unsolved mysteries. I love suspense. As a kid, I read Carolyn Keene's Nancy Drew mysteries. Maybe you did too. Did you ever read *The Hidden Staircase, Secret of the Old Clock, Intrigue at the Grand Opera,* or *The Key in the Satin Pocket?* Or perhaps you read them to your children. Many of the titles in that series over the years used enticing words to draw us into the story like *hidden, secret, key,* and *intrigue.*

Today my reading lists have changed significantly. Oh, I still appreciate the unexpected and astonishing in my story reading, and may I say I have a Book that never lets me down.

Its pages reverberate with conspiracies, theories, and knock-you-out surprises. Honestly, I have to giggle when someone comments that they just can't get into the Bible because they find it boring. I know then they haven't truly explored this Book of all books. I mean you talk about mystery and intrigue, why, the Scripture pulsates with both.

Trust me, you don't know mystery until you explore the Trinity or delve into the books of Ezekiel or Revelation. And hidden inside Scripture's onion-thin pages are ancient truths that transform lives, rescue marriages, deliver the hopeless, and redeem prodigals. The Holy Writ blows the lids off secrets as it reveals and spotlights liberating keys for our character, our conversations, and our conduct.

I am convinced that no matter where we turn in the Bible, if we ask Christ to teach us we will find truths that will stretch our understanding, illuminate our confusion, direct our path, expose our motives, and comfort us in our losses. More times than I can count, I have searched through a life like Naomi's and discovered my own bitter heart or identified with how Jonah's open rebellion led to his sinking disposition. Yes, it is true: if you seek insight, you will find it.

The opening book, Genesis, should draw in even the most reluctant as it takes us all the way back to the beginning of time. And who doesn't want to know about earth's start and our genealogy? Study the book of Genesis, and you'll find out that the Big Bang happened all right—when God spoke, and creation responded. See God form humanity out of his divine imagination and holy intentions that we might be companions to each other and be in relationship with him. And then watch some of his people—Eve, Cain, Abraham, Sarah, and Rebekah, to name a few—try to come up with their own answers to life's temptations and challenges.

"This is the history of the heavens and the earth when they were created, in the day that the LORD God made the earth and the heavens" (Genesis 2:4 NKJV).

The second book, Exodus, is one of my personal favorites. Exodus takes us on a breathtaking journey, as before our eyes a slave becomes a prince, a murderer, a fugitive, a shepherd, and a liberator. You'll be on the edge of your seat time and again as water gushes out of rock, food falls from heaven, enemies abound, rebellion turns into leprosy, and the Promised Land lies dead ahead overrun with giants.

"Who is like You, O LORD, among the gods? Who is like You, glorious in holiness, fearful in praises, doing wonders? . . . You in your mercy have led forth the people whom You have redeemed; You have guided them in your strength to Your holy habitation" (Exodus 15:11, 13 NKJV).

Midway through the Old Testament, we enter the book of Psalms, which offers believers a grand opera. It is the undulating sounds of a shepherd-king in the midst of intrigue on his best days and on his worst days. And there's something about his lyrics that resonates in our lives, like he's singing our songs. In his celebrations and in his sorrows, an aria rises and the melody captures our struggles and our successes. His music causes us to feel heard, understood, and calmed.

"He has put a new song in my mouth—praise to our God; many will see it and fear, and will trust in the LORD" (Psalm 40:3 NKJV).

Proverbs was written by the wisest and richest of kings, Solomon, who reached deep into the satin pockets of his royal robes and pulled out scrolls of daily wisdom. Sometimes I get the feeling that before Solomon started his regular regal shift in the kingdom, he slipped out to the corner café (Jacob's Jumping Java Joint) and scribbled these proverbial insights on napkins. The king's counsel feels so eclectic as he leaps from topic to topic with pithy helps for real life. Wherever he jotted them down, I'm grateful he did because those assorted truths have many times saved me from a lot of unnecessary drama in my day-to-day existence.

"Apply your heart to instruction, and your ears to words of knowledge" (Proverbs 23:12 NKJV).

The Gospels take us up a staircase of events in Christ's earthly walk that eventually leads us to the Ascension. It is exhilarating to watch his grace-filled story unfold—as Christ moves with ease in and out of the presence of his enemies, heals multitudes, performs miracles, defies explanation, challenges authority, confounds the religious order, reprimands the arrogant, and walks in the strength of humility. And Christ without apologies changes the "rules" for his people to liber-ate them.

"And when you pray you shall not be like the hypocrites. . . . But you, when you pray, go into your room, and when you have shut your door, pray to your Father who is in the secret place; and your Father who sees in secret will reward you openly" (Matthew 6:5–6 NKJV).

Philippians, written by the apostle Paul while he was incarcerated, is a book of joy. Don't you find that mysterious? It makes me initially scratch my head. I picture that kind of festive topic to be penned in a delightfully appointed hillside cottage surrounded by fragrant gardens that overlook the dancing ocean. Instead, Paul was looking at shackles, guards, restrictions, and threats. What kind of visuals are those to promote joy? I find it unfathomable that anyone could exude and write on such a celebratory subject while being unjustly persecuted. Yet as we read Paul's experience, I am enthralled with his heart attitude of gratitude in the midst of constant danger and endless uncertainty.

"Do all things without complaining and disputing, that you may become blameless and harmless, children of God with-out fault in the midst of a crooked and perverse generation, among whom you shine as lights in the world" (Philippians 2:14–15 NKJV).

There's no doubt about it, the Bible is jammed with the unimaginable. It is not a quick read but a lifelong study that will guide us down paths dappled in intrigue, where we meet people cloaked in mystery and find circumstances that defy explanation. We also will unearth keys of discovery, words of revelation, and secrets worthy of being tucked deeply inside our hearts.

Christ is the author of our stories, the hero of our hearts, and the rescuer of our souls. He knows how our saga begins and ends. He holds the secret clock of our allotted time. Neither our boisterous circumstances nor our bruised character surprises him. He continues to transform the evil intent of Satan into the mercy and goodness of God.

At the close of time when our story is told, it will be with a happy ending—all secrets revealed, all mysteries unraveled, all keys handed out, and all intrigue vanquished.

How gloriously unfathomable.

✽ ✽ ✽

*Lord, I am amazed by the story of your great grace for us, revealed in your Word. As I turn the pages of Scripture today, I praise you for giving me these reminders of your gloriously unfathomable love for me. Amen.*

# 17

# Quiet Grace

~ Nicole Johnson ~

> When He had come down from the mountain, great multitudes followed Him. And behold, a leper came and worshiped Him, saying, "Lord, if You are willing, You can make me clean." Then Jesus put out His hand and touched him, saying, "I am willing; be cleansed." Immediately his leprosy was cleansed. And Jesus said to him, "See that you tell no one; but go your way, show yourself to the priest, and offer the gift that Moses commanded, as a testimony to them."
>
> —Matthew 8:1–4 NKJV

When I read this story of Jesus healing the leper, I wonder at Jesus' instructions to the healed man. "See that you tell no one?" The man had been healed of *leprosy*. Like his friends and family weren't going to notice?

"Fred, what in the world happened to you?!"

"Oh, nothing. Just the same old, same old."

I've always been curious as to why Jesus told people he healed not to talk about the healing. And he said it often. If he healed someone or had some sort of dramatic encounter, many times he admonished that person not to tell anyone what had happened.

It hardly seems fair to have such a life-changing experience and have to keep it to yourself. And with Jesus' goal of having all men know of the love of God, wouldn't it seem he would ask those who had been touched by him to shout it from the rooftops? But he rarely did. Often the ones who had received from him did broadcast it boldly, but not because he directed them to do so. No, more often than not, he asked them to keep it to themselves.

Why would he do such a thing?

Perhaps grace is most life changing when kept to ourselves for a time.

Before a company goes public by offering their stock for purchase, it must first go through what is called a "quiet period." The SEC governs this, and during that time key executives are not allowed to talk about the company's numbers or discuss the performance of the company at all. What they have to regulate is people in the company hyping a stock before the offering. Hopefully this keeps consumers from making huge mistakes by believing in a company that might not be worth investing in.

Maybe there is a thought here worth pondering: before we go public, maybe we should first go private.

Too often in our evangelical desire to communicate the incredible grace of God, we do a disservice to that grace by forgoing any "quiet period." We miss the internal gifts that would come from having to keep something so valuable to ourselves before we share it. The idea is not that we don't ever share what God has done for us; it is that we learn some lessons in the quiet period of grace before we try to communicate it to others.

I'm not saying that we shouldn't tell others about what Jesus has done for us, but perhaps we should take the time to ponder what exactly it is that he has done before we face the world with the news. Often the pondering produces the kind of the depth that will sustain us when the public offering begins to take its toll. Otherwise, we might end up like the seed that immediately sprouts up without sending down deep roots and soon withers in the heat of the noonday sun.

Personally, I'm a little suspicious of people who come on too strongly in their communication, of anything really. Whether it's the gospel or Tupperware, I'm generally turned off by hype and overzealousness. My attorney husband is fond of saying, "When the facts are on your side, pound the facts. When the law is on your side, pound the law. When neither is on your side, pound the podium."

A second thought about why Jesus might have asked those he healed not to tell anyone about it is that he didn't want people comparing their stories or their healings. Isn't it human nature to compare? To want the same thing someone else has even though our situation might be different? Perhaps

Jesus wanted to avoid that all together, reminding us that it is *grace* that he does anything for us at all.

Grace is a one-of-a-kind experience. It's not one-size-fits-all. Remember how many different methods Jesus used to heal people? He hardly ever did the same thing twice—in fact, I'm not sure he ever did. Sometimes he used mud, sometimes a loud voice to heaven, sometimes a set of instructions, sometimes he just sent people on their way—each encounter being unique to the person and the circumstances.

A number of years ago in an original drama, I portrayed a cashier working at convenience store near a local fishing spot. About seven in the morning, an old man came into the store and got an iced tea. The man discovered upon checking out that he'd forgotten his wallet. He bemoaned the fact that he'd left it on his dresser and turned to put the tea back in the cooler. The cashier waved him out the door with his iced tea and told him she'd take care of it, and not to worry about it. On his way out the door, she admonished, "But don't you tell anybody I did that!"

About 2 p.m. that very afternoon, another man comes in and puts an iced tea down on the counter. He reaches for his money and pulls his empty pockets inside out. "I can't seem to find my wallet," he mutters a little too conveniently. The cashier doesn't even smile as she tells the young man to get on his way. He snarls at her, saying that she shouldn't be giving away iced tea if she doesn't want everyone to have it.

Maybe that cashier was a lot like Jesus. Maybe Christ didn't want to offer what he had to people who expected it. Maybe he wanted to show us that grace ceases to be grace if it is expected or demanded. It can't be calculated, predicted, or measured, or it becomes something else that Jesus wasn't offering.

Grace has to be free, unexpected, and undeserved to really be grace.

But don't tell anyone.

✿ ✿ ✿

*Father, in our zeal to tell others what you have done, don't let us miss the depth that a "quiet period" can bring. Show us how to value your grace deep inside our hearts without looking for others to validate it or us. Teach us not to compare what you have done for someone else in your generosity to what you have done for us. Free us to receive your grace exactly for what it is—a free gift, never expected or predicted. Amen.*

# 18

# Amazing Grace

~ Mary Graham ~

Receive and experience the amazing grace of the Master,
Jesus Christ, deep, deep within yourselves.

—Philippians 4:23 MSG

I came to fully appreciate my father very late in life. Until I was twenty, I just tried to stay out of his way.

Like many women, my relationship with my dad was complicated. He was gruff and irascible. As far as I know, he never actually harmed anyone in our family physically, but I don't remember a day when the possibility didn't exist. His loud, brash ways scared me and were exceedingly intimidating.

As a little girl, I'm sure I longed for my father's affirmation, but I don't remember any significant emotion for or toward him except an ever-present fear. I was afraid he'd hurt me, my mother, or one of my siblings. In reality, all he ever hurt was my feelings, but it was enough to affect me throughout my entire childhood.

During college I gave my heart to Christ, and, in the most surprising way, my feelings changed toward my dad. It was a slow change to be sure, but I began to feel more gracious and accepting toward him. For the first time in my life, I began to care about him and started expressing that in tangible ways.

After graduation, I joined the staff of Campus Crusade for Christ (which my father never quite understood), and I often traveled to different cities for various meetings and responsibilities. My dad loved playing solitaire, and in those days, the airlines gave free playing cards if you requested them. So on every flight, coming and going, I asked for cards for my father. He had more decks of cards than he'd ever need, but he delighted in my walking in the room, opening my bag, and pulling out those packages of cards. It was as if I'd won the lottery and given him the prize. Or at least that's how it seemed. And when he saw the cards, a big smile always crossed his face . . . and mine. We never really talked about it, but he knew I was thinking of him, and that was gratifying to us both.

The first time I flew overseas, Daddy was horrified that I was going to get in an airplane and head right over that ocean, all by myself. The fact that it was a ministry trip made it even worse, in his mind. Every day I was gone, I wrote a postcard home. Much to my surprise, when I returned and went to visit my parents, those postcards from all over

Europe were taped on the living room walls. I was surprised yet thrilled to see how much those postcards pleased Daddy.

The fact that I cared about my dad enough to show it in tangible ways was very new to us both. I genuinely cared for him and wanted him to know how much. His attitude toward me didn't completely change, but it didn't feel the same to me because of my concern for him. God's grace had changed me, and I now had something to give others, including my own father.

Dad still yelled at me on occasion, called me names, and frequently treated me unkindly. But I saw him in a new way because God had put forgiveness and genuine love in my heart toward him, no matter how he behaved. And the more I demonstrated love to him, the more I could appreciate other qualities in his life.

As God worked in my own heart to enable me to feel genuine care toward my dad, I started thinking about all the things I really loved in him. No one could tell a better story than Daddy, and he told them every time he had an audience. People down the street could hear us laughing hysterically.

Daddy had the most amazing mind. He never forgot anything—person, place, or thing—and all the details surrounding it. And Daddy was exceedingly generous. Although we didn't have much, what we had he was eager to share with those in need. He was an expert gardener, and his vegetable garden in the summer was a growing produce stand. Daddy supplied everyone in town with delicious tomatoes, green beans, cucumbers, and onions . . . all grown from a ten-cent package of seeds lovingly nurtured. He gave them all away generously.

Seeing these kinds of good qualities in him was new to me. I appreciated my father for the first time in my life, and I began to extend grace to him as I understood the grace that had been extended to me.

Many years later, my sister phoned to say Daddy was very ill. I traveled to see him, and the entire family was there to hear the news: the doctor had discovered stage four lung cancer. No treatment needed. No cure possible. It was a sobering moment made more intense because no one in the room had any evidence that Daddy had a personal faith in God. Though his illness had reduced him to a weak, thin, frail man, Daddy still retained a powerful presence in the room. We were still so afraid of him that no one wanted to broach the subject of his eternal condition.

Within days, all of that changed. My sister Jan volunteered to speak honestly with him about the love of God. In what felt like a miracle, Daddy responded and put his faith in Christ for the forgiveness of his sins and the salvation of his soul.

I was completely stunned. If anyone had ever been unresponsive to the love of God, it was my father. Although we didn't know what it all meant, we saw a change in his life and his spirit. He softened, and remarkably, he even regained physical strength.

To the utter amazement of his doctors and our family, Daddy lived three more years. It's not an exaggeration to say those were his best years. He became—to borrow a phrase—a kinder, gentler man. He expressed love verbally and tangibly. He seemed to care. He grew in grace.

I still can't quite get my mind around what happened. Technically, I know. Daddy's transformation is a demonstration of what the Bible teaches: when one is born again, everything changes. And although he did not receive God's gift of grace until very late in life, he is welcome at the throne of grace. That's the point, of course: salvation is not based on a lifetime of good behavior; it's based on God's infinite grace, that glorious act of redemption on the cross of Christ. I'm grateful beyond measure my father accepted that gift before he died.

It's easier to understand how God's grace saved my father from his wretched ways than to understand how God changed my own heart from fear and hate to softness and care for someone who terrified me. That's amazing grace, and I will never figure it out. I thought I could never love my father unless he changed, yet God showed me I could love my dad whether he changed or not.

The miracle in me happened first, and then God changed him.

That's amazing grace.

✲ ✲ ✲

*God, thank you for your amazing grace that saved a sinful person like me. You have transformed my life into a living demonstration of your love. I will never figure it out, but I will spend my days rejoicing in your grace and sharing it with others. Amen.*

# 19

# Mindful of Grace

~ Thelma Wells ~

Eye has not seen, nor ear heard,
Nor have entered into the heart of man
The things which God has prepared for those who love Him.
—1 Corinthians 2:9 NKJV

The United Negro College Fund has a tagline created by ad agency Young and Rubicam executive Forest Long: "A mind is a terrible thing to waste." Created in 1972 as a "plea to everybody to reject the prejudices of the past and consider the inner person," it's one of the most recognized slogans in advertising history.[7]

As I thought about this tagline the other day, I gleaned a different insight about the mind being wasted. I realize that our minds hold information from what we see, feel, taste, smell, and touch. But sometimes we seem to be out of our minds. No, not crazy. Just not thinking about what we're doing.

Have you ever driven down the freeway not really thinking about driving, unfocused on the road, thinking about something completely different than where you are and what you're doing? I have. Baby, sometimes I'm almost where I was traveling to before I know how I got there. (Maybe you don't want to be on the freeway when I'm driving.)

How many times have I done this? More than I care to admit. I've awakened out of my thoughts and daydreams only to shock myself at the distance I've driven unaware of driving at all. And then, when I realize what has happened, I get a little nervous thinking about what could have happened. One of the most perplexing mental activities is to try to figure out how I got where I was going without crashing into another vehicle or pedestrian or viaduct or building.

I've heard it said that we have three levels to our consciousness: our conscious awareness, our subconscious, and our creative subconscious. In our consciousness, we are aware of everything we say and do. Our subconscious mind cannot determine fact from fiction; it believes everything it experiences. Our creative subconscious acts out what our subconscious believes. I guess when I'm driving down the highway with my mind somewhere other than where I'm driving, my subconscious has taken the reins and, without knowing, my creative subconscious follows the lines or lane guards without concentrating on them. Do you understand how this works? I don't! I just realize that I've been protected by some phenomenon that is a mystery to me.

In my sometimes warped mind, I think that's a way grace

works. We travel down life's roads dreaming, unfocused, independent, and unaware of the dangers and pitfalls and the possible collisions around us. What we pass by is more often than not disregarded. We are not paying attention to what's ahead of us. Our focus is dulled by the sounds of the wind, the pitter-patter of the rain, or the rhythmic *thump-thump* of our tires on the highway. And somehow we make it to our destination unscathed.

Why do we get there safely? Because even when we are unfocused and oblivious to our surroundings, God is always conscious of where we are, what we're doing, how we're feeling, where we're going and what we'll meet when we finally get to our destination. Actually, if we would admit it, when we're driving like we are the only person on the highway and disregarding the safety of others as well as our own, we're asking for hurtful consequences. But God safeguards us with his tender mercy and steadfast grace. We don't get what we deserve; we get safe passage because of a good God who gives us greater benefits than we deserve.

We cannot fathom the enormity of God's grace. Our eyes are too weak to see it. Our ears are too stopped up to hear it. Our hearts are too cluttered to feel it. But God has prepared our safety even before the foundation of the world. His love acts like a supernatural bumper system guarding us against the barricades, detour signs, swerves and curves, signal lights, stop signs, and railroad crossings we must encounter on the highway to our final destination in heaven. In the vehicles of our lives, the invisible fuel of God's love is driving us, often subconsciously, to where we need to be.

As I said before, I don't understand all this. What I know is that when I get back to my conscious awareness and think of where I've come from and where I am now, the only thing I know is that I'm where I am safely without incident. That blows my mind. Immediately I thank God for protecting me and guiding the steering wheel of the car. I praise him for keeping me from colliding with other people on the road and from barreling down into the wrong lane of unsuspecting traffic. I ask for clear vision to see where he wants me to go and for discernment to understand the importance of watching out for other people who may be driving in the same unfocused condition. I ask that I may see danger lurking and darkness impending and density increasing and diversions deceiving. I pray that I will hear the sounds of stormy weather and strange echoes in my hearing speaking the instructions of the still small voice of God. As I push the accelerator of my life, I persist in pressing my way to the Love giver, and I accept, without fully understanding, the unfathomable, undeserving, and often underestimated grace of God.

I don't think the tagline for the United Negro College Fund, "A mind is a terrible thing to waste," is talking about driving down a literal road thinking about everything but what you should be concentrating on and thus endangering those around you. I think it means that it would be terrible to have a mind that is not wise, knowledgeable, or conscious of the finer things or life, full of daydreams and ignoring the Master of the universe.

I believe this tagline calls attention to the fact that we may need to put away the violations of people on the road we're driving down and instead consider their plight. This consideration should include extending people grace when they are not paying attention to what there're doing and where there're going. Forgiving them if they miss one of life's correct turns and veer in a different direction. Speaking kind words to them when they act out road rage. Offering to assist them when their fuel tank is empty and calling for help if they have an accident along the way. If they are strangers to you, they may wonder why you're being so attentive. Perhaps I would. But you don't have to give an answer or take a reward for helping; just give them what God gives you—grace and mercy.

How will your journey fare when you're blinded by your own thoughts, dreams, and circumstances? Will you detect the unmerited favor of God protecting you and keeping you safe? Or will you be deaf to the sweetness of God's tender, loving care?

You can't divert God from bestowing his grace on you, because that's a part of his nature. I suggest that you get in his safety zone by asking Jesus to come in your heart and become your permanent chauffeur so he can take over the driver's seat and give you even more grace that you can't understand. Come on. Don't wait! Let Jesus drive. Just enjoy the ride! Receive grace that is greater than all your dreams.

✳ ✳ ✳

*Master of our thoughts and minds, please open my mind and give ear to my heart's cry when I'm otherwise blinded by my own lake of vision to keep myself safe. Amen.*

# 20

# Grace Walking

~ Jan Silvious ~

Share each other's burdens, and in this way obey the law
of Christ.

—Galatians 6:2 NLT

I am an only child. Several years ago, my dad was very ill. The
four-hour drive to my parents' home was longer than I could
keep traveling on a moment's notice to care for frequent emer-
gencies. So my husband, Charlie, and I invited my parents to
move to our town. They thought about it a while and decided
that, given my dad's declining health, it would be the best move
for them and for me. Though they were a bit hesitant to leave
behind their hometown and their friends, my mom and dad,
like most aging parents, didn't want to be a burden to their child.

When moving day came, Charlie and I carefully packed
my parents' lifelong belongings, and the four of us made
the journey toward a waiting condo in our hometown of
Chattanooga, Tennessee. The journey was bittersweet as
Mother and Daddy left the known for the unknown.

The weather was blustery and rainy as we pulled into Chattanooga late that night. Every muscle in our bodies ached, and we dreaded the next day's move into the condo. But we knew it had to be done, and we were the ones to do it. We settled my parents in our guest room and fell into bed.

The weather the next morning was damp and cold—depressing weather in which to unload a moving van. The move looked like it would be a tedious mess. We glumly set about doing what we had to do when, suddenly, a welcomed brightness came in the door—it was my friend Susie, all decked out in her signature flashy clothes and gorgeous rings on every finger. I had mentioned to Susie that we were moving my parents into a nearby condo, and without being asked, she and a few of her girlfriends arrived with hammers, drills, and ladders, as well as her very handy husband, nicknamed "Big," to help with the move.

Much to our delight, before the day was over, my parents were settled in their new condo. Susie and her girlfriends had decorated their new place with things that made my parents feel at home. Their pictures were displayed on the walls of the living room, and my parents were surrounded by some of their most treasured things. Thanks to Susie and her husband, the move had gone quickly and smoothly, and my parents' need had been met with extraordinary grace.

Fast-forward five months. I hadn't often seen Susie during that time, since we both had full lives and much to do.

One of the things I had been doing was caring for my rapidly declining, often confused, very ill father. Just a few weeks after the move, he was confined to a hospital bed. His days dwindled right before our eyes. One sunny afternoon five months after he arrived in Chattanooga, he died.

That evening, after the funeral arrangements were taken care of, Charlie and I took Mother to our home, leaving behind the condo where the hospital bed and other medical supplies remained as a sorrowful reminder that Daddy was no longer with us. We dreaded going back there to clean up.

Unknown to us, however, Susie had already made plans to arrive with her moving crew early the next morning. When we took Mother back to her condo the next day, the hospital bed was removed, the medical supplies were gone, the linens were washed, and the condo was sparkling clean. A box of delicious sour cream muffins was left on the counter, along with a note reminding us that prayers were going with us as we took my dad's body back to the town we had left only five months before.

My friend Susie—"grace walking"—had been on the scene.

During the next year, we started to adjust to life without my father and tried to help Mother settle into our town, which was still unfamiliar to her. We were doing well, but obviously not as well as we thought. One morning, my mother called and asked, "What would you think if I moved back to Park Place?" Her heart's desire was to move into a retirement apartment in her hometown. Many of her friends from high school, as well as her sisters and brothers, lived there. She wanted to go to *her* home. She had moved to Chattanooga to accommodate me, but now she was ready to move back home.

I said, "Great, Mom, whatever you want to do," and I meant it. Mother and I talked about a possible timeline and arrangements for her move back to her hometown.

When I hung up, I knew just whom to call. "Susie, you aren't going to believe this. Mother wants to move back to her hometown!"

"It's okay, my friend," Susie assured me. "We can do this. Let me put the date on my calendar. I'll call my girlfriends, and we'll be there ready to move."

So move we did, one more time. And once again, Susie was there to bear the burden with me. It wasn't her mother. It wasn't her problem to handle, but because she loved me and knew I couldn't do it all alone, she was there to help and encourage me and my family.

Mother lived happily in that retirement complex for fourteen years. She relished every moment in her apartment and called it home until she went to her eternal Home. When I look back at all the moving and all the needs I could not fulfill alone, I am very grateful that I had a friend through it all who said, "It's okay, my friend. We can do this."

The wonderful grace of God is like that in our lives. Grace is what God does in us, through us, and to us that we cannot do for ourselves. God knows his children. He knows our weaknesses, and he knows exactly what we need at the moment we need it.

That is why I love this scripture so much: "So let us come boldly to the throne of our gracious God. There we will receive his mercy, and *we will find grace to help us when we need it most*" (Hebrews 4:16 NLT; emphasis added).

When we are weary and exhausted and don't know how we will make it through another day, our great God is on his throne, eager to give us all the mercy and grace we need. I remember when my parents' health was declining, so many days I just cried out "Help!" and God took it from there. He met needs that I could not have imagined in amazing ways—and one of those ways was sending my friend Susie to help us.

Susie has been the human personification of God's amazing grace to me so many times. When I was forced to handle situations that were too heavy to bear alone, there she was, with tools and helpers in tow. To me, Susie is a picture of "grace walking"—all decked out in flashy clothes, sparkling rings, and a helping hand that will not quit.

✢ ✢ ✢

*God, thank you for the "Susies" you have placed in my life to help me through some difficult situations. And help me intentionally look for ways that I can be a picture of "grace walking" to others. Amen.*

# IMMEASURABLE
## GRACE

# 21

# Missing Grace

## ~ Nicole Johnson ~

Therefore the kingdom of heaven is like a certain king who wanted to settle accounts with his servants. And when he had begun to settle accounts, one was brought to him who owed him ten thousand talents. But as he was not able to pay, his master commanded that he be sold, with his wife and children and all that he had, and that payment be made. The servant therefore fell down before him, saying, "Master, have patience with me, and I will pay you all." Then the master of that servant was moved with compassion, released him, and forgave him the debt.

But that servant went out and found one of his fellow servants who owed him a hundred denarii; and he laid hands on him and took him by the throat, saying, "Pay me what you owe!" So his fellow servant fell down at his feet and begged him, saying, "Have patience with me, and I will pay you all." And he would not, but went and threw him into prison till he should pay the debt. So when his fellow servants saw what had been done, they were very grieved, and came and told their master all that had been done. Then his master, after he had called him, said to him,

"You wicked servant! I forgave you all that debt because you begged me. Should you not also have had compassion on your fellow servant, just as I had pity on you?" And his master was angry, and delivered him to the torturers until he should pay all that was due to him.

—Matthew 18:23–34 NKJV

Stephanie wasn't sure how she'd gotten herself into so much debt. Little by little, she guessed, just like every other sticky situation she'd been in. However this one would not be solved so easily. She had a good job and she made good money, but now she found herself on the opposite end of demanding phone calls for minimum payments. She contemplated filing for bankruptcy but didn't know how she'd explain the situation she was in. After all, she still had some pride.

This is just the situation that Jesus described in Matthew 18 as he told the parable of the unforgiving servant. There were no credit card companies, no banks offering no-interest loans, and no opportunity to file Chapter 7 and start over. The man in his story was indebted to the master, and the master wanted to be paid. We don't know if the man was irresponsible with money or if he'd just fallen upon hard times. We don't know if he had a family he was looking after or if he was just loose with his resources. Whatever the case, he was in the same kind of trouble.

Stephanie got off the phone with one of the credit card companies and was satisfied with her explanation. She'd told them the truth (with a little twist) that her mother had been in the hospital and she'd gotten overloaded with responsibilities. The kind voice on the other end of the phone said she understood—in fact, the voice mentioned that she was losing her mother after a long battle with cancer and she knew what it was like to feel so much pressure. Stephanie felt relief when she hung up and immediately vowed to pay off that card as soon as she was able. Having been given more time, she decided to get to work collecting the money that was due to her.

Which is exactly what the unforgiving servant did. He had no means to pay the king back the amount of money he owed, so he was about to be thrown in jail. He fell to his knees and begged the king to give him more time. He promised he would repay the debt. The story says, "The master of that servant was moved with compassion" (Matthew 18:27 NKJV). Probably because the man was foolish enough to think he could actually repay the debt. And then the master released the man and forgave him.

I have wondered, if the man asked for more time and the king released him, what might the man have thought he got? I think perhaps more time. Which is how the foolishness continued.

Both Stephanie and the unforgiving servant thought that with more time they could get back on their feet, pull themselves up by their own bootstraps, and take care of the problem. But that was the problem in and of itself, wasn't it? More time wasn't going to solve the problem any more than more time can save a sinking ship from sinking farther. But both of them kept trying simply to keep their heads above water, bailing water out bucket by bucket.

The man begged for more time, and the king gave it to him. Stephanie asked for more time, and the kind woman gave it to her—but each missed the grace in the transaction. The king granted forgiveness to the man, but he missed it. Stephanie got her extension, but she took the grace the woman gave her for granted. Therefore, neither had any grace or forgiveness to give to others when they were called upon. Each was too busy calculating his balance and points to acknowledge that the ledger had been cleared.

Neither of these is a story about money. Jesus used the physical example of money and the practical application of what we all know and understand to try to teach us a spiritual lesson. It is a parable about grace and the kingdom of God.

If we miss the grace of God in our own lives, we have no grace to give anyone else. How busy are we calculating what others owe us while forgetting to look at the balance that has been paid for us? If we don't first see what God has done for us—that he has offered us unmerited favor—we can never offer any unmerited favor to anyone else.

The gift of unmerited favor was so important to God and

so contrary to the way we think that Jesus had to try to explain it many times. He used many different stories with lots of different characters to continue to challenge the conventional thinking of the day. The kind of thinking, by the way, that is still conventional today. The kind of thinking he consistently tries to break through to teach us about grace—unmerited favor.

We know all about merited favor. We're really up to speed on that. It's the unmerited version we have such a hard time with. We all fall into thinking that with more time we can work out our problems, pay our debts, deal with our issues, and so on. But often, time is not the problem, and more of it just keeps us in denial about what the real problem is—us, and our way of thinking.

How difficult is it for us to let others pay for things for us? To let the ledger be completely one-sided? Most of us feel terrible about that. And for some who don't, who always seem to be looking for others to pick up the tab, they are often the ones who are the least generous with others. How well we do with receiving grace definitely determines how much grace we give to others.

Grace refuses to be measured, calculated, portioned, or controlled. The moment we try to put unmerited favor into those kinds of terms or measurements, we are in danger of missing it altogether. And who would want to miss the favor and blessing of God?

✻ ✻ ✻

*Father, teach us more about your unmerited favor. Teach us to receive it and allow it to change our lives. Let it free us to be more generous with others, to forgive their debts, and treat them with compassion—as we have been treated even more generously by you. Show us how to walk in the grace that you have extended to us so that we might extend it to others. In your name and for your sake. Amen.*

# 22

# Measuring Up

~ Patsy Clairmont ~

These things I have spoken to you, that in Me you may have peace. In the world you will have tribulation; but be of good cheer, I have overcome the world.

—John 16:33 NKJV

How do you measure up?

When I measure up, I get sixty inches of height if I stretch my neck and tilt my chin(s). When I was a kid, I loved to have my measurements taken and would have announced if possible on national TV my ongoing attempt to be taller than my 4' 10" mom. When I finally passed her height by a whopping two inches, I bloated with boast.

Today I feel different about anything that measures me. For instance, I break out in scales if I have to be weighed. And don't waste my time trying to measure my waist because I'll have to belt you if you get too close. Even my shoe size is a "boot," since my foot has more sole at this juncture. Everything seems to get fluffier as you, uh, season.

It's interesting to me how many things and ways we measure: houses by square footage, trips by miles, days by hours, oil by barrels, blood by units, and animals by herds, packs, flocks, litters, gaggles, and so on.

*Gaggle.* Isn't that a great word? It sounds like a cross between giggle and gag, which is what I do when I think of my age. We usually gauge age not only by years but also by hair color, wrinkles, and vigor. My Mamaw (grandmother) lived to be ninety-seven and a half . . . now that, girlfriend, is a lot of calendar pages to gaggle over.

Even when I was a child, Mamaw's face looked like an ancient map, one that I loved to trace in my mind. Little did I realize that her map would one day lead me to my own mirror. Today I have the joy of being a crumply map for my grandchildren.

Take heart if you are a kindred weathered-faced friend, because wrinkles turn to crinkles when you're joyful. And who doesn't love a well-patterned smile?

But there are things in life one can't measure easily, like our appetites. We try measuring how hungry we are with words on a scale from *sorta* to *ravenous*, which reminds me of an article I read recently about a hot-dog-eating contest in New York. The young man who won ate forty-nine hot dogs in twelve minutes. Twelve minutes? Gulp. Groan.

Another thing that is difficult to measure is love. Oh, we measure people's behavior and then try to determine what that says about their love. Behavior can be an indicator of intentions or maturity, but love itself defies precise dimensions. I hold my arms up toward the heavens trying to show my grandchildren how much I love them, but that falls short of describing the fullness of my feelings. And even harder to explain is God's love.

We are told in Ephesians 3:19 that the love of Christ passes knowledge. Try as we might, there is no sundial, dipstick, Geiger counter, thermometer, yardstick, stethoscope, blood pressure cuff, or seismograph that we can use to measure God's love. It just can't be done.

That's hard for us to grasp. I mean, I don't know about you, but my love bucket gets holes in it and runs dry from time to time. My heart left on its own narrows, which is why I need access to the resource of God's love to widen and deepen my capacity.

In the book of Exodus we watch God's love protectively and provisionally cover his people with his presence. We hear God's thunderous voice through a burning bush, on a mountaintop, and through his spokesman, Moses. We observe God's discipline through plagues, hunger, and thirst. We are aware of his generosity as he provides manna, water, and a promised land. Then we try to measure what all that means about God, about us, and our relationship with him. And from our ponderings of God's Word, we decide what we believe about our life of faith.

I noticed every time the Israelites in Exodus went through a struggle, they would attack Moses, wondering if God had deserted them. It's hard not to feel abandoned or take it out on others when we measure our happiness according to our comfort levels. Life has the capacity to cramp our style. For Moses' crew it was a tedious path and treacherous enemies that made them wiggle and whine in discomfort, while for us it's escalating gasoline prices, high taxes, broken relationships, and war.

When we use happiness as a measure for our sense of safety and peace, our tally comes up short on how we thought God would come through for us. In another words, our numbers and his love don't seem to jive.

For years, I kept thinking if God loved me he would rescue me out of my difficulties. There have been those times, but often he doesn't. I have been left to wade through high waters in low boots, which caused me to puzzle over God's love and scramble about to figure out faith.

Then as I delved deeper, which is one of the benefits of hardship, I realized that God tells us again and again in Scripture that "in the world [we] will have tribulation" (John 16:33 NKJV). Quite honestly, I just didn't want to believe it. I want life to be easier not only for me but for all those whom I love. Yet I have observed that change seldom occurs without struggle, whether it's a caterpillar wiggling free of his cocoon to fly or a person squiggling free of addiction to rise with new-found liberty.

Look in the Old Testament at Joseph's life—rejection, harassment, and injustice. And what was the result? A wise man came forth out of the prison, one who rose up to handle the responsibility of being second in command over the most powerful nation in the world at that time. Somehow Joseph was able to trust God's love regardless of being locked in a cell for an offense he didn't commit.

When I have to sit long in a doctor's waiting cell—I mean, office—I get whiny. I can't imagine Joseph's years in a dank, creepy room without peanut butter or Nick at Nite.

I have to remind myself when times crowd in with pressure, when people hurt my feelings, when my job loses its appeal, when my children fail to heed my advice, and when the newspapers read like doomsday reports, that God didn't promise life would be easy but that he would be with us as Buzz Lightyear (children's hero) would say, "To infinity and beyond!"

God can take a jail sentence and use it for the good of the prisoner, whether we are incarcerated behind iron bars or emotional ones. He uses our rejection issues to tutor us in the importance of compassion and inclusion. And harassment is just the right material to teach us the importance of knowing who we are in Christ, so we are not intimidated or persuaded that we are hopeless.

So today if you are wondering how you measure up, rest assured that God is on your side. And if you are trying to figure out God's measurements, know that his love is beyond knowledge. Try as we might, we cannot fully comprehend the immeasurable love of God—although one of the indicators is Jesus.

✿ ✿ ✿

*God, thank you for your promise that you will be with me, no matter what. Today, instead of spending my time and energy trying to measure up to others' expectations, I choose to rest in your immeasurable grace and unconditional love for me, expressed in your Son, Jesus. Amen.*

# 23

# A Matter of Perspective

~ Carol Kent ~

They will speak of the glorious splendor of your majesty,
and I will meditate on your wonderful works.

—Psalm 145:5 NIV

The e-mail was warm and inviting. A friend I had been out of touch with for several years was now in ministry leadership in a large church in Calgary, Alberta. She asked if I would come to Canada to lead a communications seminar at the church and then speak at a women's retreat they were hosting in the mountains. We confirmed a late May date that worked well on both of our busy schedules. In truth, I thought I was doing a favor for a friend, but God had another idea.

My husband, Gene, and I arrived the day before the seminar and enjoyed working with enthusiastic participants nonstop for the next two days. As soon as the event ended, Gene and I jumped into our rental car to make our way down the highway to the foothills of the Canadian Rockies for the weekend. Snowcapped mountains captivated my attention as mile after mile provided postcard-perfect images of God's glorious creation.

We had been told it would be not be uncommon to see bighorn sheep on the steep cliffs, a lynx chasing a hare (for the purpose of grabbing a quick lunch), an elk grazing in a remote meadow, a deer and her fawn drinking in one of the pristine lakes, or even a group of grizzly bears fishing in a fast-moving stream. The ride to our destination did not disappoint as we observed wildlife and nature against the landscape of the Creator's colorful, textured canvas. The farther into the foothills we drove, the bigger the mountains appeared—and the smaller my personal problems became.

I don't know exactly when it happened, but God ministered to me very personally amid his immeasurably spectacular creation that weekend. I found myself singing in the car with gusto, "Then sings my soul, my Savior God to Thee, how great Thou art! How great Thou art!" Gene joined in, and we belted out an impromptu duet—realizing the enormity of the creation demanded a vocal response.

Arriving at a resort in Kananaskis County, Gene and I found ourselves in a nature preserve so large that it encompasses three national parks. From our room we could see aspen groves, dry grasslands, towering snow-covered peaks, and rugged foothills. A little red bird decided to perch on the railing around our deck, and he provided private concerts on each day of the retreat. The fireplace in the room warmed my body and my heart as I realized how much my soul ached for a respite from the pressure, busyness, and exhaustion I had been feeling. In the middle of this wilderness, I felt the presence of my Creator God.

It was Saturday afternoon. Though I had spoken three times to a responsive group of attentive participants, I suddenly realized God's purpose in bringing me to this place—it wasn't so much for *me* to minister to others, but for *him* to minister to me. Gene had already left on a hike up the mountain, so I decided to spend some time alone with God. My heart was drawn to scriptures that describe the immeasurable, extensive, indescribable wonder of our God and of his glorious creation. I picked up my Bible and read some of my favorite verses and then cross-referenced them on my computer to see how various translations captured the essence of each scripture:

- "On the glorious splendor of Your majesty and on Your wonderful works, I will meditate" (Psalm 145:5 NASB).
- "O LORD, our Lord, how majestic is your name in all the earth!" (Psalm 8:9 NIV).
- "So we will not fear when earthquakes come and the mountains crumble into the sea" (Psalm 46:2 NLT).
- "And blessed be His glorious name forever; and may the whole earth be filled with His glory. Amen, and Amen" (Psalm 72:19 NASB).

Gene and I had been experiencing a deep personal disappointment that bordered on despair. Our son is incarcerated with a life-without-the-possibility-of-parole prison sentence. Only weeks before our trip to Canada, our attorney had called with disappointing news: "Gene and Carol, I am sorry to tell you that all of the requests we have made for evidentiary hearings and appeals have been rejected at both the state and federal levels. There's nothing more our legal firm can do to help your son."[8]

My method of coping was to bury myself in my writing and speaking. I thought that if I could just work hard enough, I'd be so exhausted when bedtime came that I would fall asleep instead of giving in to the depth of grief that threatened to swallow my joy. It was a way of running away from my negative thoughts, my personal pain, my fears for my son, and my agonizing grief.

That day in the wilderness, God did a new thing in my heart. As I gazed on his immeasurable greatness in creation, I heard him whisper to me the words of Jeremiah 32:27: "Stay alert! I am GOD, the God of everything living. Is there anything I can't do?" (MSG).

I thought about the women I had met during the retreat. Some of them were in the middle of their own impossible circumstances:

• Brianne was from South Africa and had fallen madly in

love with a ruggedly handsome Canadian when he was visiting her country. He promised to love her forever, but now, two children later, after moving her across the ocean away from her family and friends, he announced he was a homosexual and no longer loved her. Brokenhearted, she poured out her sadness and confusion. She wanted to know: "How could God have allowed this to happen?"

• Jill was a young mother of two who said, "I just want to live my life for things that matter, but I'm stuck in a small town with almost no ministry opportunities. I believe God has called me to speak and to be involved in leading Bible studies, but I feel like I run into a closed door every time I try to use my gifts."

• Becky expressed her love for her autistic child, but she admitted there were days when she wondered how she could cope with her son's physical and emotional demands. She wondered if she would ever have a life free of caring for a child with so many special needs.

• Jodi was dealing with secondary infertility. She was grateful for and deeply loved her one beautiful child, but since that healthy birth she'd had three miscarriages. She longed for another baby. She told me, "People just don't get how painful this is. They say I should be happy with the child I have—and believe me, I am—but I long to have more children."

After praying individually with several of these women, I returned to my room, realizing I wasn't alone in my longing for different circumstances than my family was experiencing. Gazing at the magnificent view outside my window, I could almost hear God say, "Is anything too hard for the LORD?" (Genesis 18:14 NLT).

In this place so far from home, God was adjusting my perspective. I found myself embracing my new kind of normal. Then I read: "For I am about to do something new. See, I have already begun! Do you not see it? I will make a pathway through the wilderness. I will create rivers in the dry wasteland" (Isaiah 43:19 NLT).

At that moment, the little red bird on my railing began to chirp with gusto—reminding me that if God cares about the birds of the air, surely he has not forgotten me.

✿ ✿ ✿

*Father, I sometimes think I have a better plan figured out for my life than what you have allowed. When my circumstances feel overwhelming, help me to look at your glorious creation and know that you are all-powerful, almighty, all-wise, and immutable. I hang my weakness on your immeasurable strength. Amen.*

## 24

# An Unending Supply

~ Sheila Walsh ~

On the third day a wedding took place at Cana in Galilee. Jesus' mother was there, and Jesus and his disciples had also been invited to the wedding. When the wine was gone, Jesus' mother said to him, "They have no more wine."

"Dear woman, why do you involve me?" Jesus replied. "My time has not yet come."

His mother said to the servants, "Do whatever he tells you."

—John 2:1–5 NIV

Have you ever found yourself at the end of a particular day thinking, *Well, I had no idea when I woke up today that by tonight my life would have changed so much.*

Perhaps you just discovered that you are going to be a mom, and as you lie in bed that night, reflecting on all the implications of this small piece of gigantic news, you know that you will never be the same again. Or perhaps the news you received was not happy news: "Your cancer is back." As those words rattle around your head and your heart, you wonder what tomorrow will hold.

One day can change the landscape of a human life. I think that had to be especially true for those who first followed Christ. Each day brought fresh revelation, startling miracles, unusual behavior, or disturbing statements—but it all began in an unlikely place: at a wedding. We know the story from Sunday school. It's the first miracle Jesus performed, turning water into wine. Have you ever asked yourself why he did it? Was it just to please his mother? Did he know the family well and want to spare them the embarrassment of being the one family that year whose wedding was ruined because of defective catering? I think it was much more than that.

A wedding is always an occasion to celebrate, but in a small town like Cana it could only be described as an event. Cana is set high up in the hills of Galilee about nine miles north of Nazareth. Jesus and his mother and friends were invited to the celebration. The event of the wedding and Jesus' first public miracle is linked to the previous chapter by the words "on the third day," or "three days later." When you read chapter 1 of John's Gospel, you get a sense of how early this wedding miracle is in the unfolding of Jesus' ministry. He had just begun calling men to follow him. Andrew, Simon Peter, Phillip, and Nathaniel had dropped what they were doing and, three days later, found themselves included on the guest list at the wedding. At that time they knew very little about Jesus, for all these events took place in less than a week.

It's not quite clear how these new friends ended up on the wedding list, but as Nathaniel was from Cana, he may have helped facilitate that.

Andrew had initially been one of John the Baptist's disciples, but he had been there on the side of the Jordan River when Jesus passed by and he heard John declare, "Look! The Lamb of God who takes away the sin of the world!" (John 1:29 NLT). So Andrew left John that day and followed Jesus. He and an unidentified friend spent the day with Jesus, and at the end of the day Andrew's only priority was to find his big brother Simon Peter and tell him the radical news that they had found the Messiah.

When we think of the word *Messiah*, we think about Jesus being the Christ, God's anointed one. But the Jews, who had waited for centuries, had a far different picture of who would come than the carpenter's son walking by the Jordan River. The Old Testament portrays the Messiah as one who will put an end to war and injustice and who will save his people from their sins.

The Jewish people were living under Roman law, which was oppressive and demanding. Some of their own had been recruited by the Romans to extract taxes from their fellow Jews. They could demand as much as they wanted as long as Rome got its lion's share. Like those given special treatment in concentration camps, if the Jewish tax collectors cooperated with the Romans, these men were often more cruel than the authority they represented. A small amount of power can often corrupt a human heart.

So the Jews waited for Messiah, the one who would come and put all wrongs right and rescue the chosen ones from their tormenters. Then after four hundred years of silence, as Malachi penned the final word of the Old Testament, God began to speak again.

First came John the Baptist, preparing the way for the One who would come. Those who were longing for the Word of God to be revealed followed John, but there was more. The news began with a whisper:

*Did you hear?*

*Can it be true?*

*John said the sign is real.*

*Messiah has come!*

So they followed Jesus, waiting to see what he would do. Would he quietly gather an army and then establish God's kingdom? What will he do first? They watched and waited and found themselves at a village wedding. Everything was flowing beautifully until the unthinkable happened—the hosts ran out of wine. That would be hard enough in a large city, but in a small town the humiliating stigma would cast a pall over the whole wedding and the newlyweds.

Mary must have been close to the family since they confided in her that they were in trouble. So she came to Jesus. He responded to her, "Woman, what does your concern have to do with Me? My hour has not yet come" (John 2:4 NKJV).

Jesus' words to his mother reflect the fact that he recognized this was not a mother coming to a son for help, but a believer coming to God's chosen one for a miracle. Mary submitted to Jesus and said no more to him. There was no pleading or manipulation; she simply told the servants to do exactly what Jesus said.

Jesus told the servants to fill six stone jars with water. Each jar would have held twenty or thirty gallons. When the servants took the first jar to the master of the feast for tasting, the master wanted to know why they had kept the best wine for last.

Now, why did I choose this miracle to expand on immeasurable grace? Of all the miracles of Christ, this would seem the least life-changing. It was fabulous for the family that everyone went away talking about how lovely the bride looked and wasn't that wine amazing, but is that all? No, there is so much more.

Here is what I believe the gift of this miracle is to us today. The servants brought their empty jars to Jesus, and he told them to fill them with water. In other words, we bring to Jesus what we have. Then Jesus filled the ordinary water with his power, transforming it into something wonderful. Not only that, but the volume produced was one hundred to one hundred and fifty gallons, more than they could possibly need.

This miracle is about so much more than an embarrassed host, rescued by Jesus. It is a sign to us. That is what the word *miracle* means here. It means a sign. Turning the water into wine was a sign to the disciples, who must have talked about it all the way home. It was a sign to Mary that just as the angel said, this boy of hers would be great, the Son of the Most High God (Luke 1:32). It is a sign to you and to me, that Jesus is who he says he is and that he can take our ordinary lives and transform them with his grace.

Do you feel a little empty today? When you look at your life and what you have to offer, does it seem too ordinary, almost embarrassing? Not to Jesus. This day there is grace available to fill and transform your empty or weary heart, and it will not run out. Bring your emptiness or ordinariness to Jesus, and your heart will not be able to hold all the grace poured out in you!

✡ ✡ ✡

*Lord, thank you for including this sign in your Word so that I can know for sure that you are who you say you are and that you can take my ordinary life and transform it with your immeasurable grace. Today I am bringing my emptiness to you, ready and eager to experience your overflowing grace! Amen.*

# 25

# Grace: Fullness of Life

~ Marilyn Meberg ~

Here I am! I stand at the door and knock. If anyone hears my voice and opens the door, I will come in and eat with him, and he with me.

—Revelation 3:20 NIV

Grace is difficult to adequately explain or define. It requires instead a picture, an example, or a story that illustrates rather than pinpoints a specific meaning. Jesus did not attempt to define grace, but he daily illustrated it when he was on earth. His entire life was a picture of grace and an invitation for all of us to enter into and receive his grace.

But just what exactly does that mean? How does one enter into his grace? What does it mean to receive his grace? I by no means know all the answers to the many and varied questions we have about grace, but there's one thing I know for sure: *I need it*. In fact, I desperately need it.

In her short story "The Fulness of Life," Edith Wharton wrote that a woman's life is like "a great house full of rooms," most of which remain unseen, "and in the innermost room, the holy of holies, the soul sits alone and waits for a footstep that never comes."[9]

Dare I impose upon the magnificent writing of Edith Wharton? If I did, I would suggest her "woman" is every woman. It is every man. Initially, we all sit alone waiting. Many do not know what they are waiting for; they just know they "need" it. Whatever the "it" is, they wait in silence for it to appear. Perhaps the "it" will take away the loneliness, the barrenness of the house full of rooms.

A gazillion years ago when I was working on my master's degree in English, I took a night class entitled Great American Authors. Edith Wharton was one of the authors we studied, and her short story "The Fulness of Life" spawned a lively discussion one night. What exactly is the woman waiting for and why? Had she been abandoned by a faithless lover, or perhaps was she waiting for something or someone who had yet to appear in her world? Or maybe the footstep was a call to purpose and meaning in her life . . . a meaning never made clear, a call never heard.

As the discussion swirled about, I suggested what I just wrote in this devotional. The "woman" is a picture of all persons who wait for someone or something to fill the room and take away the emptiness. My comment was acceptable to my classmates until the professor asked for my opinion about who or what the something or someone might be, not only for the story's woman but for anyone else sitting and waiting in life. Talk about a setup! Preach, Marilyn!

Soon after my short "sermon," the class had our fifteen-minute break. A young woman named Vanessa and I often took our breaks together. We were both pregnant with our second baby, we both drank herbal tea, and we were both taking one class a semester for no other purpose than to have one night a week talking to someone without a pacifier in his mouth. As I poured the hot water over her citrus mint tea (we took turns supplying the "surprise" bag each week), she giggled at me and said, "Marilyn, you're so quaint." I looked at her in amazement. "Quaint? I'm not old enough to be quaint. I'm only twenty-six!" Vanessa went on to explain that maybe I wasn't quaint, but my ideas about God and the need of a Savior to enter every person's room and supply salvation, purpose, and meaning was very quaint.

As the semester progressed, I learned Vanessa had what she described as a "passing acquaintance" with God, but nothing serious. She waited behind the door for his footstep. In fact, she learned at the end of the semester that her husband was having an affair, and Vanessa's Tuesday night class had given him a perfect opportunity to be with the other woman. My heart broke for her. She became even less interested in my "quaint" ideas about God and his availability to cushion the blows of life. On the last night of class, she hugged me and said, "Let's stay in touch." We didn't. I never learned if her marital brokenness was mended, and she never learned my baby lived only fifteen days. We both needed grace.

Grace was offered to me in the words of 2 Samuel 22:31–33:

> God's way is perfect.
> All the LORD's promises prove true.
> He is a shield for all who look to him for protection.
> For who is God except the LORD?
> Who but our God is a solid rock?
> God is my strong fortress;
> he has made my way perfect. (NLT)

I have spent years struggling to believe God's ways are perfect when they don't feel perfect to me. But by the same token, I have experienced him as a solid rock. I have felt his "strong fortress" nature holding me and protecting me from unbelief and abandonment. I also believe his promises are true. Jesus told the disciples, "I am with you always, even to the end of the age" (Matthew 28:20 NLT). I think one of the greatest examples of his grace to me is that he allows me to be weak in front of him . . . to falter occasionally in my faith and ask why. He doesn't leave when I do. That is a way I enter into his grace.

The greatest way to receive God's grace is to respond to his "footstep" outside the door. The scriptural metaphor is not a footstep, but a heart knock. I love the gentle image of Revelation 3:20: "Look! I stand at the door and knock. If you hear my voice and open the door, I will come in . . ." God's grace never skips a room . . . never fails to knock. We don't sit alone inside a meaningless house with too many rooms unless we choose to.

God's grace offers a Savior who paid the sin-penalty. When we realize the penalty for the sin into which we were born is death and that Jesus paid that debt by dying on the cross, we come head-on into grace. Amazing grace!

God's grace is doing what I am unable to do for myself. I can't wash myself clean of the sin stain; only Jesus can, and he did. I can't provide the hope of heaven for myself; only Jesus can and he did. I can't provide a life full of meaning and purpose; only Jesus can, and he does. I don't have faith to believe "all things work together for good" (Romans 8:28 NKJV) except as he enables my faith and he does.

Not only does God's grace provide the removal of sin through Jesus and the sure knowledge I'm heaven-bound when the time comes, but I also have God's grace for my daily bumbling about that is not always a good witness. I fail others and I fail myself. I look bad to others and I look bad to myself. That does not faze God. He does not turn away mumbling that Marilyn was a poor investment. Instead, he delights in me. Zephaniah 3:17 says he rejoices over me with joy. Who would do that? God! Why?

The most liberating dimension of grace is this: when you and I receive the grace of God through Jesus, we become brand-new persons. We are no longer seen by God as bumbling persons dropping occasional bad witnesses. Ephesians 4:24 says we have a "new nature, created to be like God— truly righteous and holy" (NLT ). Colossians 1:22 says Jesus "has reconciled you to himself through the death of Christ in his physical body. As a result, he has brought you into his own presence, and you are holy and blameless as you stand before him without a single fault" (NLT). That, sweet baby, is grace!

☆ ☆ ☆

*God, today I will respond to your gentle knock and open wide all of the rooms of my heart so that you can infuse them with your amazing, liberating grace. Amen.*

# 26

# Many-Colored Grace

~ Jan Silvious ~

As each one has received a special gift, employ it in serving one another as good stewards of the manifold grace of God.

—1 Peter 4:10 NASB

When my boys were young, I loved to buy them Garanimals! These shirts and pants could be coordinated by matching the animal on one piece of clothing to the same animal on another. I could always count on the colors being compatible and the boys looking as if their mother were very successful at dressing her little gentlemen. With three boys close in age, that can be a feat! Whenever my sons wore their Garanimals outfits, I loved the fact that they were coordinated and even seemed to act as if they thought they looked good!

I guess I was probably sensitive to that kind of thing on a deeper level because when I was about five, I remember an outfit I wore that just didn't go together. I can see it in my mind to this day: the blouse was light blue with hand-smocking across the front. The skirt was wool, pleated, and red-and-green plaid with straps that came across the shoulders. The blouse and the skirt were pretty, but they didn't match and I was highly aware of that fact. I was so aware that I remember crying and telling my mother how I disliked it. What I didn't realize was that was all I had to wear for dress-up. Money wasn't abundant, and that was my dressy outfit.

As I have grown older, I have discovered that there are other "matching" issues that are far more significant than a blue blouse and red-and-green-plaid skirt. When I began to dive into a deeper understanding of the grace of God, I realized it was all about matching: God matches his grace to our needs. I discovered a scripture that describes this concept so well. In his first letter, the apostle Peter encourages us, "As each one has received a special gift, employ it in serving one another as good stewards of the manifold grace of God" (1 Peter 4:10 NASB).

As I began to study this verse, I was fascinated by the word "manifold." While this verse is about how we each have received spiritual gifts from God and how we are to exercise them in serving one another, it makes reference to a broader description of grace. It speaks of "manifold"—or many-colored—grace, indicating that God's grace is custom-designed for whatever your need might be. If you have a blue need, his grace will be blue. If your need is a green need, guess what color his grace will be? You've got it. It will be the perfect hue of matching green. God's grace is all about supplying the very thing that you need—not something like you need or something that will do for now, but the exact answer you need for the moment. I love that about God. He knows us perfectly, loves us eternally, and is incredibly involved in giving us strength and supply in our moments of weakness and want.

The book of James tells us: "Consider it a sheer gift, friends, when tests and challenges come at you from all sides. You know that under pressure, your faith-life is forced into the open *and shows its true colors.*" (1:2–4 MSG; emphasis added). Many-colored trials are met with many-colored grace, so in the end as you endure, you will be perfect and complete, lacking in nothing. That's what God offers to us when we are at our weakest point.

That's why the apostle Paul could boldly say that the Lord told him, "My grace is sufficient for you, for power is perfected in weakness" (2 Corinthians 12:9 NASB). God demonstrates his unconditional love for us in various ways in order to meet us where we are, in order to show us he is interested not only in one part of our lives but in whatever our concerns might be. That is his amazing and wonderful grace.

One of the memorable experiences of walking with the Lord is the way he comes alongside and personally meets us where we are. I've asked him to show me where a lost contact lens was hiding and had him direct my gaze to a dusty spider web in the crevice between the porch and a step. I've called out to him for intervention when a real estate transaction was going bad, and I've seen him intervene. I've asked for peace in situations where peace wasn't humanly possible, and he has wrapped me in his incredible, calming peace.

Both of my parents went through serious, extensive surgeries during the years before they died. As their only child, I had huge emotional investment in being supportive not only to the one having surgery but also to the one who was waiting for news. I found that very hard and often longed for a brother or sister to call or to at least share the burden of "being there." Since that wasn't my reality, I learned that God had an "only child with elderly parents" grace that just fit my situation. Looking back, I can remember the lonely vigils, but even more, I can remember the all-encompassing peace that God gave. It was a peace his grace provided in days and especially nights when fear and sadness wanted to move in. What I needed he quietly provided, and when I walked out of those trials, I recognized the tint of his grace touch. He had been there and had left his color-matched fingerprints all over my struggles.

I personally experienced the touch of God's grace in a way I won't forget. I found out I had to have a heart catheterization one day and entered the hospital the next—which happened to be my birthday. It was two days before Christmas as well. The situation seemed surreal, but the presence of that many-colored grace was unmistakable. It was if God knew I needed to know he was there. I needed the grace of his presence. I can look back and remember all the peace that surrounded me as the nurses in the catheterization lab sang "Happy Birthday" and as I was rolled back to my room with Christmas carols playing in the halls. God let me know in so many gentle ways that he knew where I was and that he was there with me.

In every kind of life event, from inconsequential to potentially life-altering, God has eagerly given to me from his abundant supply of unconditional, uniquely designed, always available, many-colored grace.

This immeasurable, many-colored, custom-designed grace is yours when you invite the Lord of the universe to take up residence in your life. He loves to give grace to those who receive him, no matter what color grace you need!

✯ ✯ ✯

*Lord, no matter what specific need or struggle I have today, I will call out to you with confidence, knowing that you will answer me and meet my unique need from your abundant supply of unconditional, immeasurable, many-colored grace. Amen.*

# 27

# Nudges of Grace

~ Luci Swindoll ~

Friends come and friends go, but a true friend sticks by you like family.

—Proverbs 18:24 MSG

I grew up in a family that loved to visit. We told stories, acted out conversations in various dialogues or dialects, played instruments, and were involved in competitive games. Those who weren't performing were sitting in the audience egging on the rest of us. There was no television back then, of course, so this kind of visiting was the precursor of "the tube" in our house.

Probably the most gregarious visitation occurred during family reunions. My maternal grandmother was the ringleader. She dreamed 'em up, decided when we'd go, called everybody, planned meals, and assigned beds. Every summer, without fail, our whole gang of relatives went to Granddaddy's little bay house in south Texas for a week. It was a lot of fun, and I have the pictures to prove it. As one of the kids, I often slept in a tent or on a cot in the backyard under the stars. We'd build bonfires and tell fishing stories late into the night until we all fell asleep.

Everything we did spoke of connectedness. My parents put a high premium on that, and we grew up with those kinds of family dynamics. Everybody wanted to be connected to the rest of the family.

Interestingly, I'm not so much that way now. Having never married and lived alone for thirty-five years, I've come to appreciate (and sometimes prefer) being alone. Many of my friends are social butterflies, but I'm not. They get their energy from other people, while I get mine from solitude. Personally, I think the "better" way (if I can put a value judgment on it) is to be more social. I believe that's God's way. His love, mercy, and grace are for *all* people, and he frequently has to remind me of that fact. I could hole up in my house for days and days and be very happy, so God does things that nudge me to get out of myself and reach out to others. When I do, I'm ever so grateful and he rewards me for having done so. I call these little nudge rewards my *grace moments*. They sometimes sneak up on me. They might be solitary, such as spending time with one of my nieces instead of reading the book that's calling me from my bedside table. Or they might come in bunches like what happened earlier this year.

During a thirty-day period in the spring of 2007, I had three reunions with friends I hadn't seen in decades. And each was totally unexpected. Not once did I have a clue I'd ever hear from them again or have the opportunity to visit for a while. They were uncommon gifts of grace from God.

The first one was with Carol Kenny Williams, whom I'd not seen in fifty years. Carol and I used to go to the same church in Houston. She's a very accomplished pianist and always accompanied me when I sang solos in that church. I moved from Houston to Dallas in 1957, and from that time on we've not kept in touch except through reports from our mutual friend, Ney Bailey. Carol married Jimmy Williams, had a family, and together they ministered for years with Campus Crusade for Christ.

As God would have it, my dear friend Ney (who also works with Crusade) knows Carol very well, so she asked if I'd like to have lunch with her and, if so, she'd arrange it. I was thrilled. We invited Carol to come to my home where four of us (Carol, Ney, Mary Graham—president of Women of Faith and formerly with Campus Crusade—and I) spent several hours together reliving old times, enjoying a delicious meal (another gift from Ney), laughing our heads off, and catching up on the years between us that had fallen through the cracks. It was an unforgettable experience, and I'll treasure that day forever. It was a *grace moment*.

The second encounter was with Bill and Jerre Simmons, a couple I'd not seen in forty-seven years. I had no idea where they lived or if they were still living . . . and I never dreamed their home was only thirty miles south of mine. Jerre used to be an English teacher and Bill, a radio announcer, but they've both retired now. Out of the blue, Jerre wrote an e-mail to Insight for Living in search of my whereabouts, and it was forwarded to me for a response. We started writing back and forth, and before long we were planning lunch together.

We met at a Dallas restaurant, and I got there first. Thinking perhaps they might not recognize me after all these years, I waited in the lobby area for their arrival so I could see them as they drove up, wondering if they'd changed as much as I. When they walked in, they came directly to me and said smilingly, "We'd know you anywhere." In a matter of minutes, it was as though no time had lapsed between us. Another *grace moment*. We were seated, ordered lunch, and visited for several hours. We had so much fun recalling old times, old friends, everybody's whereabouts, and sweet reminiscences. Since then, we've been trying to get the next visit on our calendars.

The third reunion was with a wonderful former pastor of mine, Dr. Dwight Pentecost. Dwight teaches at Dallas Theological Seminary and helped officiate at the burial services of both my parents. For forty years, he's been my mentor and friend, but I'd not seen him in thirty of those years. I'd gone to the Good Friday service at the church where my brother Chuck pastors, and lo and behold! Dwight Pentecost walked into that service and asked Chuck (who happened to be in the foyer) where I might be sitting. When I recognized Dwight, a million memories flooded over me. I cried. Our time together was a complete *grace moment*. What a gift to have him there. He sat by me during the service, and afterward we had the sweetest visit.

I'm glad I paid attention to the nudging of my heart in those instances because I so enjoyed the connection with all these friends from yesteryear.

It's been said, "When the heart speaks, the mind finds it indecent to object." There are times I feel very self-sufficient and don't need anyone else. God has to remind me that he has a better way for me. He calls me to companionship, to connectedness, to reunions. And I'm grateful he does. It's easy for me to be too independent. So much so that I forget I've been made for fellowship and service.

If God didn't give us unexpected opportunities to reach out to others whether we wanted to or not, where would we be? As my friend Anne Lamott says, "I do not at all understand the mystery of grace—only that it meets us where we are but does not leave us where it found us." I don't want to be left where grace initially found me. I want to grow up in Christ, be his servant, and show others what grace is like.

✯ ✯ ✯

*God, thank you for the many opportunities you give me to reach out to others—even when I don't feel like it! Continue to show me you did not create me to be independent and alone, but to connect in a community and to share your grace with others. Amen.*

# 28

# He Giveth More Grace

~ Mary Graham ~

> When times are good, be happy;
> but when times are bad, consider:
> God has made the one
> as well as the other.
>
> —Ecclesiastes 7:14 NIV

Life is hard. When exactly I learned that I'm not sure, but I've known it a very long time. Jesus himself put it this way: "In this world you will have trouble" (John 16:33 NIV).

My mother, thirty-six years older than I and the mother of seven children when I arrived, lived thirty-four years after I was born. There are few lives I've known, or studied, as well as hers. She was marvelous.

When she was only sixty, which is my present age, Mother started showing signs of what we much later learned was Alzheimer's disease. I'd never heard the word when her diagnosis was delivered.

She lived ten years with the disease, which took something from her every single hour of every single day during those years. If getting what you deserve in life is the way the game is played, she would have been the last one, at least in our family, to lose everything. It started with her keys, then the words in her sentences, then the memories she held dear, then the recognition of her loved ones, then her mind, and then her ability to care for anyone, including herself. In time, she lost her bodily functions and finally her life. It was a painfully slow and agonizing process.

There were a few lighthearted moments like the time she forgot how to get out of the bathtub. The two of us got so tickled, and I can still laugh just thinking about it. It's quite amazing, actually, that I didn't drown us both. It was her last real bath.

Sadly, she knew something was wrong almost from the beginning. At first, she would laugh at her forgetfulness. ("Did you say you wanted coffee or iced tea?" she'd say for the umpteenth time and we'd both laugh hysterically.) But one day, walking down the sidewalk on a beautiful day, holding my hand like she'd done when I was a child, she said to me, "Honey, I think there's something wrong with my mind." I wasn't sure whether to believe her, until she said a few minutes later, "I think that's our house." We were blocks away from the street where she lived.

Those days are long ago and far away. Mother died more than twenty-five years ago. Now the disease is commonly understood and often discussed. I never hear the word, however, without feeling an agonizing pang inside.

Those were the hard days of my life. Unmanageably hard. No one knew what to do to help my mother. And although there was nothing we could do about her condition, everyone in the family had to do everything for her. We were responsible for my parents all the time for almost ten years. Sometimes I wonder how we made it through. And then I remember.

In the words of Chuck Swindoll in his magnificent book that is now a classic, we needed a "grace awakening."[10] Every day required new grace. Every moment it was grace that got us through. And the grace never ran out. It was amazing, boundless, and infinite. In fact, God's grace during that time was infinitely more than I could ever have imagined and more than I can almost believe looking back.

When it was time to make decisions, we needed grace. Wisdom and understanding helped lead us to the right decision, but every decision was too hard to make apart from God's grace. Should we leave Mother at home? Should we arrange for her to live with one of us? Should we put her in assisted living? What about Daddy? He wanted her with him as they'd always been, but of everything she'd painfully lost sight of, perhaps the most challenging was that she'd forgotten who daddy was. After fifty years of marriage, she didn't like "that man" who came in her room every night. And sometimes she got angry when she saw him get in her purse! He was dying of cancer at the time, and if we'd taken her from him, it might have killed him. If we didn't, it would cause her horrible angst. The situation was dreadful, but moment by moment God gave us grace.

When our patience ran out, we had grace for the moment. It would be hard to imagine anyone loving a mother more than we loved ours, but there were days so frustrating I could not bear her behavior. I wanted to shake her shoulders and make her understand reality. But just when I thought I couldn't take the next step, there was God's grace—calming me and giving me the strength to do the next thing.

When we grew impatient with one another and each sibling felt as if his or her burden was greater than the others', we found grace to forgive and to keep going. My siblings and I tried to take turns caring for our parents, relying on the grace that only God grants so we could give it to one another. Otherwise our responsibility truly was unbearable.

My mother was a hummer. She hummed *all* the time, and one of the tunes I became the most familiar with from her humming was a great hymn written by Annie Johnson Flint entitled "He Giveth More Grace." It goes like this:

> He giveth more grace as the burdens grow greater.
> He giveth more strength as our labors increase.
> To added affliction, He addeth His mercy;
> To multiplied sorrows He multiplies peace.

When we have exhausted our store of endurance,
when our strength has failed when the day is half done,
when we reach the end of our hoarded resources,
Our Father's full giving is only begun . . .

His love has no limits
His love has no measure
His power no boundary known unto men
For out of His infinite riches in Jesus,
He giveth, and giveth and giveth again.

My mother hummed that tune all my life; I can hear it now in my head. But during those days, the words of the tune became words of life to me. When I didn't feel relieved, I found relief in the reality of this hymn.

God's grace is immeasurable. What an amazing reality. It is the constant solace of my soul. Somehow, though, I'm not sure I would ever have known that if my life had not been so hard those many years ago. From a distance, I now see those days as a gift. Those were the days my mother's faith became my own in a deeper way and my father actually came to faith in Christ. We became family in the truest sense of the word as we learned what it meant to love, not merely in word but also in deed. We learned courage and strength as we laid down our lives for our mother, and in many ways, we found the meaning of life.

Life can be hard. But God's immeasurable grace will see you through.

✻ ✻ ✻

*Lord, even when life is hard, I will rest in your unfailing love and care for me. As the song says, out of your infinite riches in Jesus, you give and give and give again your immeasurable grace to me. Amen.*

# 29

# Resting in Grace

~ Sandi Patty ~

Find rest, O my soul, in God alone;
my hope comes from him.

—Psalm 62:5 NIV

Those of us who live in cold climates and have school-age children understand the significance of the two-hour snow delay. It is the best. Let me back up and describe winter in Indiana for a moment. It is very dark and cold in the winter. The days are short. The kids actually go to school *before* the sun comes up. Something is very wrong with that. You get used to it, but it is still very weird. Then it gets dark very early in the afternoon, like around five o'clock. Because it is so cold, the kids are inside most of the winter, and this honestly drives us all crazy. By the time winter is coming to a close and spring is approaching, we are pretty much sick of each other and have a severe case of cabin fever.

During the winter months, the kids walk around tired

most of the school day. Quite honestly, I don't know how they do it. I certainly couldn't.

Anyway, just when you think you can't get up at 5:45 a.m. one more day and get the kids motivated, fix breakfast, fix lunches, do hair, sign papers for the teacher, and all the myriad things that have to happen before your kids head off to school—you wake up and turn on the TV to get the weather so you know how to dress the kids for the day. But, then, there it is. Like a gift from heaven . . . the ticker that runs continuously at the bottom of the TV screen, announcing the school districts that will be delayed (or even closed) due to bad weather. I reach for my glasses so that I can clearly see each and every school name that goes by. Because our school district is Anderson Community Schools, we are always at the beginning of the alphabetical list. So I wait, through the S's, and the T's. On into the W's and V's. Ah, we are getting to the end of the alphabet and our name should appear soon. *Here it comes . . . Oh please, God, let there be a delay today.* And just as I think that, I see it. As I blink back the tears, I read, "Anderson Community Schools—2 hour delay." What that means is, the kids will have the same bus schedule and same school routine, just delayed two hours.

This is a gift from God. Everyone gets to sleep in for some much needed rest, and the kids go to school in the daylight. It's awesome. After I do my little two-hour-delay celebration dance in the kitchen, I get the awesome task of going to our kids' rooms and telling them that they get to stay in bed for two more hours. This is a delight all its own because the reactions, although varied, carry the same message: *We are not worthy! We are so grateful!* It's hilarious. I love walking into Erin's room to quietly say, "Erin, it's a two-hour delay today," to which she will respond in a grateful, "Yes!" Or Jenn will say, "Praise God" or "Thank you, Jesus." Donnie will say, "Are you serious?" or Aly will say, "I am so happy." Jon will gather up the animals—he sleeps with three dogs—and explain to them that they don't have to get up yet. I think Anna has been known to shed a tear or two. It's great. Sometime, I want to remember to take my camcorder into their rooms when I tell them this awesome news.

It is the coolest thing to know that God will always give us just what we need when we need it. Never early, never late, but just when we need it. That two hours of extra rest does so much for all of us. Sometimes we don't need a month's vacation, just a two-hour delay—to which we can reply in a grateful, "Yes!"

✡ ✡ ✡

*Lord, thank you for always giving me just what I need, when I need it. And even during life's unexpected delays, I will be grateful for the opportunity you have given for me to rest in your immeasurable grace. Amen.*

# 30

# Refining Grace

## ~ Thelma Wells ~

And He has said to me, "My grace is sufficient for you, for power is perfected in weakness. Most gladly, therefore, I will rather boast about my weaknesses, so that the power of Christ may dwell in me. Therefore I am well content with weaknesses, with insults, with distresses, with persecutions, with difficulties, for Christ's sake; for when I am weak, then I am strong.

—2 Corinthians 12:9–10 NASB

My friend Lynda gave me a book in the late 1990s that was life changing for me because it showed me the grace of God through the eyes of the authors. My entire perspective of serving God and working for the kingdom was transformed from just being a servant of God to being a servant to God as well. It spelled out the significance of doing what I was called to do. It altered my perception of what the judgment seat of Christ will look like when our works will be tried in the fire before our Lord Jesus.

Romans 14:10–12 says, "For we will all stand before God's judgment seat . . . So then, each of us will give an account of himself to God" (NIV). 2 Corinthians 5:10 tells us, "For we must all appear before the judgment seat of Christ, that each one may receive what is due him for the things done while in the body, whether good or bad" (NIV). In the context of both scriptures, it is clear that the judgment seat of Christ involves believers giving an account of their lives to Christ. The judgment seat of Christ does not determine salvation; that was determined by Christ's sacrifice on our behalf (1 John 2:2), and by faith in him (John 3:16). All of our sins are forgiven and we will never be condemned for them (Romans 8:1). We should not look at the judgment seat of Christ as God judging our sins, but rather as God rewarding us for our lives.[11] Understanding what the judgment seat of Christ is, this story in Rick Howard and Jamie Lash's book *This Was Your Life!* turned my life around.[12] Rick had a dream that he went to the judgment seat of Christ and was surrounded by people he knew. When it was his time to stand before the Lord, he thought he would be rewarded as the pastor of a megachurch and having fame in the media that surpasses many. He stepped up to Jesus sitting in the Judge's seat and presented his works.

Jesus tried Rick's works in the fire—and they burned and burned and burned until nothing was left but a deep, black hole. The pastor stood there with a broken heart and asked

Jesus why all of his works were burned because he had worked for the Lord all his career. Jesus told him that, no, he had not worked for the glory of God because God had told him to go into ministry on foreign fields. But because his wife refused to marry him if he went, the pastor had selected the woman over God. He had been responsible for millions accepting Jesus and for many great and wonderful works, but because the pastor did not accept the real calling of God and instead pleased his wife, his works were burned up like wood, hay, and stubble. Sure, the pastor entered into the kingdom of God in heaven, but he lost his rewards for the work he did on earth.

Rich also saw an old lady of no acclaim. Someone who was never written up in the paper, never appeared on television, did no radio interviews, and never spoke for a conference of any size. As she walked up to the judgment seat of Christ and presented her works to Jesus, they begin to burn. When they finished burning, what was left were stacks of gold, silver, and precious stones. This nobody on earth was rewarded at the judgment for edifying people while glorifying God. She received the rewards that Jesus will bestow at his judgment seat.

As Rich stood before the judgment seat waiting for Jesus to talk to him, there was a period of total silence and no activity. Disappointed and wondering, he woke up from the dream with no precise results.

I cried and cried after reading this story. I asked myself, "What if I worked all my life thinking I was working for the right cause for the right reasons only to find that I had worked in vain?" How awful it would be to think that you are working for the glory of God to find out too late that you've deceived yourself for decades.

As I lay on the bed weeping, I began to worship God for loving people enough to show them a glimpse of what the consequences are when you work the works of him who sent you, even if you do so for the wrong purpose. There is no way that I can express my gratitude to God for his immeasurable grace written through the chronicles of this book. What a God we have to share one of the mysteries of the working for God without the baggage of doing things to be counted great among the people of earth. I learned that day that I must work for eternal value—nothing more, and nothing less. So I asked myself, how can I value the God of everything who has made everything for his pleasure? My answer includes his words:

*Do not be conceited.*

*God's grace is sufficient in times of trouble and affliction.*

*The power of Christ rests upon you.*

*Be content with weaknesses, insults, hardships, persecutions, and calamities for Christ's sake.*

*Know that when you are weak, God is strong.*

*Glorify God in all your ways.*

Folks, this is the kind of grace that cannot be measured. God's grace has no limits. His favor has no boundaries. His love has no borders. There is no compromise in God. God's grace is ours without asking for it. Everywhere we go, everything we do, every relationship, and every activity is covered by God's grace. When things are going haywire in your life, it's grace that keeps you from losing your mind. When financial problems seem to persist in your life, it's God's immeasurable grace that keeps you from going under.

When your health fails and you can't get well, its grace that keeps you in perfect peace and restores your soul. This grace allows you to walk through the valley of the shadow of death without fearing evil. When your loved one dies and you think you can't live without him, it's God's grace that sustains you and keeps you on your feet. When you've lost your job and can't seem to find one that can support your lifestyle, it's God's grace that puts someone or some business on your mind and gives you the plan to succeed.

When your relationships are in an upheaval and your communication is faulty, it's God who shows you how to conquer that situation. When your church is reeling from hurt and shame, it's God's grace that picks you up and turns things around and puts your feet on solid ground. In the face of wars and rumors of wars and people you care about are fighting on foreign fields, it's God's grace that stabilizes you and builds you up for the task of waiting. When you've made an unthinkable mistake and everyone else seems to set you aside, it's God's immeasurable grace that speaks forgiveness into your spirit and revives you again. Look at every situation in life that you can think of and view the immeasurable grace of God towering over us all.

Who would not long to live in eternity with a Savior and Redeemer whose love is so overwhelming, mercy so far-reaching, and favor so accommodating that they would give up their personal agenda to satisfy God's? Our personal agenda as we work for the kingdom of God is not to satisfy ourselves with gladness and boasting about what we are doing for God, but to glory in the cross of Jesus, develop a meaningful relationship with him, and give him all glory and majesty for everything, every act, every deed, every work we are doing. We are anointed to serve the Lord with gladness, never serving ourselves because of his immeasurable grace.

✡ ✡ ✡

*It's all about you, Lord. Help us to know that it's not about us! The kingdom of God is your kingdom, and we have inherited from you our positions in your kingdom. Thank you for allowing us to live with you forever while totally submitting to you while on this earth. Amen.*

# ETERNAL
# GRACE

# 31

# Forever Grace

~ Patsy Clairmont ~

I trust in the mercy of God forever and ever.
—Psalm 52:8 NKJV

Throughout the forty-five years Les and I have been married, he has bestowed upon me many gifts both wonderful and wacky. The fox-y jacket was dreamy, except I was so allergic I couldn't even be in the same room with it, much less wear it. We actually had to pull off on the shoulder of the freeway to put the jacket in the trunk so I could breathe. Good choice, wrong girl. Then there was the horsehair purse. Let me just say that gift fell deeply into the well of wacky. Although when I wasn't sneezing, I was laughing. A gift should bring joy . . . right?

Along with the myriad gifts, Les usually presents me with two cards, a funny one and a romantic one. Isn't that sweet? The funny one usually highlights one of my annoying qualities (like my telling him how to drive). Not so sweet. And the romantic one talks about how he will love me forever . . . Aw, I like that.

But here's my question: what is forever?

Therein lies a human dilemma: to explain the unexplainable. We can't measure eternity by what we know, because we physically die and that would appear on all practical levels to be the end of that. But (aren't you glad there's a but), not according to Scripture, which assures us that life goes on into and for eternity.

When I want to get across to someone how painfully difficult something was, like a tedious trip, a flat-as-a-pancake mammogram, or a long traffic signal, it is like me to quip, "It lasted forever." What an absurd statement, but I'm not against a little absurdity if it helps drive home the extent of my frustration, which is why we throw in "forever," isn't it?

Have you ever had a day that felt like forever?

Me too.

Recently I had an endoscopy and a colonoscopy. I think the doctor's intention was to meet in the middle. Actually since I was out cold for the tests, that time went quickly. It was the preparation that I wasn't sure had an end to it. No pun intended. Honestly, trying to chug the preparatory meds felt like a never-ending process, when in fact it was over in a matter of hours.

How many times have we read a story that ends with these words: "And they lived happily ever after?" Yet we all know that's a big fat fairy tale because life is tough, people spat, princes leave, princesses grow weary, hearts are broken, and health is tentative. It's not that there are not also blessings, joy, and love. Oh, and did I mention hope? Hope brings us full circle back to forever. Not the I-wish kind of hope, but the I-risk-my-life-on-it hope.

In Luke 13, there is an account of a woman who was bent over. She had been staring at the ground for eighteen years. Imagine that. Scripture tells us, "She was bent over and could in no way raise herself up" (v. 11 NKJV). Eighteen years . . . and then one Sabbath day she was in the synagogue when Jesus was teaching, and everything changed. Jesus "saw her" (v. 12 NKJV). I love that phrase. And he called her to him, and Jesus healed her. "Woman, you are loosed from your infirmity" (v. 12 NKJV). And in that moment she stood upright and began praising God.

Wouldn't you just love to talk with that woman over a Starbucks latte? I know I would. I have a feeling she would tell me that those eighteen years felt like forever. But I think she would also tell me that when she stood upright and looked into the eyes of Christ, her definition of *forever* changed . . . forever.

I think the first question I would ask her is why she didn't cry out to Christ for help. Many accounts have folks crowding Christ for healing and pleading for mercy, but she was in his presence and never said a word. Not a single word. I wonder after eighteen years of looking earthward, had she given up hope? Was her heart was as downcast as her body? Did she not dare allow her hopes to rise up lest they be dashed once again by her bent body? Or had she decided this was to be her lot in life and she had not considered there was a way out of her brokenness?

You see why I need to have a jolt of java with this girl-friend? I've got questions. *What did it feel like to finally stand straight? How did others treat you when you were bent over? What did people say after your healing?*

As I've been thinking about this woman, I couldn't help but think of myself. I have osteoporosis, which is affecting my posture. I have to constantly remind myself to stand tall and sit straight, but it's a real effort to get these old bones to comply. It bothers me because I've always had such good posture, so I cannot imagine the depression experienced by this woman who was bent over for so long.

But it isn't just physical issues that cause us girls to lower our gaze, is it? I wondered if this woman didn't cry out to the Lord because she felt unworthy? Was she guilt ridden or full of shame? Shame is weighty and will keep our eyes downcast and will keep us from asking for help even when it's available.

Perhaps some of us have become so accustomed to our "infirmity" that we just make room for it rather than reaching out for a resolve. Or maybe we have relational issues that are a stumbling block to intimacy. We are not likely to open our hearts with those toward whom we are harboring hurt. There will always be a reserve, a bent-ness, in the way we interact with them. We will find our gaze dodging theirs. Relationships are weighed down by our collections of resentments.

I was made infirm by guilt because of my mistakes as a mom. I wanted to do everything right as a parent, and while that was a worthy goal, it was a foolish expectation. God is the only perfect parent. I was a young, immature, insecure, and emotionally unstable woman, which fed into my parenting attempts. I didn't realize my overprotectiveness, high expectations, and innate negativity was harmful, but of course it was. I realize that now.

To forgive oneself is a huge step in standing straight. It's very humbling to admit one's parental failure. Humility initially feels scary, but it breaks the cords that bind us to our failure and allows us to walk tall as we step into God's grace, whereas shame weighs down our spirit and keeps us tied to our mistakes. Humility brings hope; shame brings bleakness.

The first step in forgiving ourselves is a willingness to let go of our failure—failure is not our friend regardless of how much time we've spent together. Don't cozy up with shame; it Velcros itself to our identity to keep us from experiencing the litheness of God's Spirit.

I don't know what weighs you down and keeps your vision restricted from all God has, but Christ sees us in the crowd and calls us to himself for divine purposes. He would not have us downcast or disabled by our fears and failure;

Christ knows our needs and the burdens that weigh us down. He is touched by our heart-cry and moved to compassion on our behalf. Boundless grace is in his touch . . . it is his gift to us, the forever-after kind!

✡ ✡ ✡

*Lord, when I feel bent down under the weight of shame or failure, I will cry out to you. Help me to forgive myself and to accept your free gift of forever-after grace. Amen.*

# 32

# Grace Beyond Rules

## ~ Jan Silvious ~

I will give you a new heart, and I will put a new spirit in you. I will take out your stony, stubborn heart and give you a tender, responsive heart. And I will put my Spirit in you so that you will follow my decrees and be careful to obey my regulations.

—Ezekiel 36:26–27 NLT

Grace can be scary to those who only feel secure when there are a lot of rules. One of the main objections to grace goes something like this: "If you don't have rules to tell people what to do, they'll be lawless and do whatever they want to!" Of course, what these "rule people" fail to consider is that folks do wrong things whether there are rules or not. Unless there is something inside to direct a person toward doing the right thing, having outer rules is not going to make a person do what is right. In fact, sometimes having a lot of rules just brings out the lawbreaker in us.

I spoke at a conference several years ago that was held at a small retreat center. This quaint camp had a long history of owners, and it had a lot of antique furniture and equipment on the grounds. It was really a lovely place—except for the signs placed on everything from the fence to an old wood stove in the lobby that said, DON'T TOUCH! Everywhere I turned, DON'T TOUCH! stared me in the face.

As I encountered these signs, at first I thought, *They are really proud of their stuff.* And then, I thought, *What is the problem with touching?* And then I thought, *I have to touch something!* So I waited until I was alone with an antique cast iron pot . . . and I touched it! There was no reason other than the fact that there were so many signs telling me not to touch it. So everything within me said, "Touch it!"

No harm was done. The pot survived the touching, and I didn't get turned in for going against the rules. However, not every situation is like that. Sometimes, obeying the rules is critical, especially when it comes to God's rules.

In his Word, God has given us some essential rules to make our lives easier and to bring order to our existence. Just a few of these include: don't lie; don't steal; don't kill; don't commit adultery; honor your parents. There are more, but you catch my drift here. All of these rules are good for us. God gave us those rules because he loves us.

There is only one problem. Just as I had to touch that black cast iron pot, we've all "had to touch" something off limits, and as a result, we are all guilty of breaking God's laws. God isn't pleased when we break his laws, because his rules are for our good. However, he also knows we need help in dealing with our penchant to break laws "just because."

That's where grace comes in. We can find this kind of grace dramatically played out in the story of a woman caught in adultery. Let's pull back the curtain and take our seats as we watch this drama unfold.

At dawn he appeared again in the temple courts, where all the people gathered around him, and he sat down to teach them. The teachers of the law and the Pharisees brought in a woman caught in adultery. They made her stand before the group and said to Jesus, "Teacher, this woman was caught in the act of adultery. In the Law Moses commanded us to stone such women. Now what do you say?" They were using this question as a trap, in order to have a basis for accusing him.

But Jesus bent down and started to write on the ground with his finger. When they kept on questioning him, he straightened up and said to them, "If any one of you is without sin, let him be the first to throw a stone at her." Again he stooped down and wrote on the ground.

At this, those who heard began to go away one at a time, the older ones first, until only Jesus was left, with the woman still standing there. Jesus straightened up and

asked her, "Woman, where are they? Has no one condemned you?"

"No one, sir," she said. "Then neither do I condemn
you," Jesus declared. "Go now and leave your life of sin."
(John 8:2–11 NIV)

Isn't that a gripping account? Can't you feel the tension?
The "rule police" had busted the rule breaker, and they wanted
the Teacher to condemn her and make her pay. They wanted
to stone her, to make an example of her to prove that if you
break a rule you are as good as dead.

But Jesus, who was full of "grace and truth" (John 1:14
NIV), handled the incident in a way that shocked everyone, not
the least of whom was the woman who knew she was
doomed. She knew the law had been broken. She had done it!
She was guilty. I can only imagine that she was grasping at her
clothing trying to cover herself while bracing her body against
the expected blows of the stones. Like everyone, I'm sure she
knew that there were rules, and there were consequences.

What the woman didn't know was that she was standing
in the presence of Grace himself. She had no idea that Jesus
was any different than the other men standing around until
he stooped down and wrote on the ground. We don't have
a clue what he wrote, but the time he took squatting down
gave the stone throwers a chance to think it over. Maybe
she wasn't the only one who was guilty. Maybe they needed

to rethink what they were about to do. Maybe, maybe, maybe . . .

We don't know what the Pharisees were thinking, but this much we know: they dropped their stones and walked away. The guilty woman and her equally guilty accusers had just experienced God's incredible grace.

The woman was probably the only one who realized this grace because she knew she was in need. There was nothing she could do to make her situation right. She had no power within herself to change what she had done. I can only imagine the relief and gratitude that welled up in her soul when Jesus told her, "Neither do I condemn you. Go now and leave your life of sin" (John 8:11 NIV).

That day, Jesus set her eternally free from the penalty of her sin and told her there was a new life waiting for her. Don't you know that gave her a new heart attitude? Can't you imagine that everything within her had been changed? Her life had been spared, and by God's grace, she had been set free to go and sin no more.

The choice was still hers. No law could keep her from returning to her sin, but grace could. Jesus spared her life, removed any condemnation, and pointed her in a new direction. The woman had broken the law, but God's grace set her free from paying the penalty. The law was still a good law, a righteous law that applied to everyone—but the grace of Christ had not only spared her earthly life but had also given her a new and eternal life, one in which she would have the inner desire to make better choices.

Once you have experienced God's grace, keeping the law is no longer your goal. Wanting to please the One who has taken away your condemnation and set you on a better path becomes your driving motivation. That's why the "rule police" don't have to worry about those who understand grace. The desire to keep the law and please God is written in their hearts.

✢ ✢ ✢

*Lord, I agree that the rules in your Word are good and true and right. But sometimes I can't resist breaking those rules "just because." In those times, I am so grateful for your eternal grace, which takes away all my sin and inscribes in my heart the desire to please you. Amen.*

# 33

# Grace for All People

~ Mary Graham ~

For God so loved the world, that He gave His only begotten Son, that whoever believes in Him shall not perish, but have eternal life.

—John 3:16 NASB

Marilyn and I had not really known each other personally until we ended up traveling together for a couple of weeks in Africa. When I first met Marilyn (at the airport, as I recall), I remember thinking, *Well, she is the cutest thing I ever saw.* And she was—a darling little blonde, born and bred in Alabama, with characteristic Southern charm. She, like I, had never been to Africa, and we were beside ourselves with anticipation.

It was 1984, and Marilyn and I were traveling with about ten other young women who served on the staff of Campus Crusade for Christ. We worked on campuses in the United States from Tuscaloosa, Alabama, to Berkeley, California, and had been invited by the leadership team of the African Campus

Crusade for Christ to come to the continent. Each of us was assigned to spend a couple of weeks on major university campuses in Africa. We flew to Nairobi and split in teams of two to go to Uganda, Zimbabwe, Malawi, South Africa, and Kenya.

Marilyn and I were assigned to the University of Zimbabwe, located in Harare, the largest and most populated city in the country. We arrived on a Saturday afternoon and spent the following week with the Campus Crusade staff. We had meetings, appointments, and wonderful conversations with so many people we grew to love.

Marilyn spoke with such a Southern drawl that I spent my whole trip being her interpreter. In Zimbabwe, everyone speaks the King's English with the most sophisticated accent. Marilyn's version of the language sounded nothing like theirs. Almost every time she spoke, all eyes turned immediately to me. They were far too proper to say it, but their expressions said it all: *Huh? What did she just say?* They were fascinated with her, and as the days went on, their fascination turned to love. They didn't speak the same "language," but somehow their ability to communicate was not at all deterred.

We spoke of the love of God to those university students and, as if we were E. F. Hutton, they listened.

And here's the most memorable part of the week: the university students we met were very responsive to the gospel. They were interested in us as Americans but far more interested in this God of love we know. They wanted to know him too. They asked, "Does he know us? Does he love us? Does he care? How do you know this?"

I've been in Africa many times since then. The last time I was there was on a trip with Women of Faith and World Vision. The experience was vastly different from my 1984 adventure with Marilyn and the students. This time, we were in Kenya to contribute help and hope to some of the world's neediest children. Despite the differences in these trips, two things were completely unchanged: my love for the people and our need for a language interpreter. Only this time, I was not the one translating from a Southern drawl to proper English; I needed a translator.

In Kenya, we met a grandmother named Rebecca who, by the world's standards, has nothing. Absolutely nothing. She is responsible for providing for her grandchildren since her daughters died of HIV/AIDS. We visited with her in her tiny, unfurnished mud hut. There was barrenness all around—not a material possession anywhere in the room. She lived with the children in this small hut void of any material possessions. Children for whom she was solely responsible were running around everywhere. Rebecca had a huge responsibility on her shoulders, but she was a picture of love, grace, freedom, and peace. She seemed untroubled by what would to me be absolutely overwhelming circumstances.

There were many lines in her beautiful face, but I sensed no cracks in her good humor. Our team experienced an immediate connection with her in our hearts, though our languages prevented any verbal exchange. We spoke to someone in English, who spoke to someone in Swahili, who spoke to someone in a tribal language, who spoke to Rebecca on our behalf. It took a little time for our verbal expressions of love and encouragement to reach her, but once they did, her face beamed and her smile reached from one ear to the other.

Just before we left, I asked Rebecca how we could pray for her. My question went from one interpreter to the next, but her answer needed no interpretation. She smiled broadly, shook her head in delight as if I'd said she had won the greatest prize on the planet and said again and again, "Asanti, Jesus! Asanti, Jesus!" The interpreter told us she said she needs nothing. She thanks Jesus for all he's given her. For once in my life, I was completely speechless.

We came to give to these people, yet we left on the receiving end. Because of the amazing effectiveness of World Vision, we are assured that Rebecca will get basic essentials: clean water, food, education for her grandchildren, and medication when they need it. She now has hope, and her little ones have a future. But during our brief time together, she gave us what memory does not erase: a picture of who Jesus can be to someone whose heart trusts in him. To borrow the words of an old hymn, "Nothing in her hands she brings; simply to the cross she clings."

Both of these times I visited Africa, and every time in

between, I have been struck by the universality of the gospel. I've often heard there is common ground at the foot of the cross, and it's true. Regardless of language, lifestyle, heritage, or country of origin, the love of God is for the whole world. God's eternal grace is enough for everyone. He's got the whole wide world in his hands.

And God's grace is infinite. Not only is it enough, it is more than enough—for here, for now, and for all of eternity. His grace is enough, and more than enough, for every person on the planet, to all who receive it. No place on earth, regardless of how remote, is too remote for his grace. No people group on earth, no matter how unique they appear to us (or we to them), escapes the provision of his grace.

God's Word is clear: his grace is universal—for all people, in all places, for all time. Everyone on earth needs God: "For *all* have sinned and fall short of the glory of God" (Romans 3:23 NASB; emphasis added). And everyone on earth is loved by and provided for by God: "For God so loved the *world,* that He gave His only begotten Son, that *whoever* believes in Him shall not perish, but have eternal life (John 3:16 NASB; emphasis added).

We will never fully understand the heart of God, but every now and then he gives us glimpses of his grace in people, even in the remotest part of the earth.

God's grace is sufficient. For all people, in all places, for eternity.

✲ ✲ ✲

*Lord, you created every person in this world, and you desire for everyone, everywhere, to experience your infinite, eternal grace. Truly you are an amazing God! Show me today how I can be a partner in spreading the good news of your grace to the ends of the earth. Amen.*

# 34

# Sheltering Grace

~ Marilyn Meberg ~

For you are my hiding place;
you protect me from trouble.
You surround me with songs of victory.

—Psalm 32:7 NLT

One Christmas, during my Lonely Acres era, Dad, my dog Pugsy, and I set out to find a Christmas tree we could cut down and drag home. There were a gazillion perfect fir trees growing on our forty acres of property, but something in me did not feel satisfied with any of them. Not wanting to settle, I asked Dad if we could just keep looking a bit longer.

And then, there it was . . . the perfect tree. Because of my unbridled enthusiasm Dad chopped down the tree, but he was confused. "Marilyn, why this tree? It is so poorly shaped . . . one side is missing at least five branches. We'll have to hide that huge hole by placing it against the back wall." I had no idea why this poorly shaped tree won my heart, but it did.

Decorating the tree took place in a near-perfect Hallmark card environment. We drank hot chocolate, watched the softly falling snow, and were warmed by a roaring fire in the fireplace. The only non–Hallmark card element was Pugsy's peculiar behavior. She sat utterly transfixed as the tree was being decorated. We all took note and wondered.

When we finished our evening meal and returned to the living room, at first there was no sign of Pugsy. Then I spotted her. With careful maneuvering, she had managed to drag her little plaid cushion bed under the Christmas tree where the hole was. She and her cushion filled the hole perfectly. It was as if that "tree hole" had been carved out especially for her—not too high, not too wide; it was just right. If ever I've seen a dog smile, Pugsy smiled throughout that Christmas season.

Years later when Ken, the kids, and I would go to the Christmas tree lot (usually one in front of a grocery store), everyone understood why Mom always looked for a slightly misshapen tree.

I wonder if my years-ago desire for an imperfect tree was simply an awareness of not being fully shaped myself. I was too young to understand that I, like Pugsy, needed the solace of a tree hole. I love the image in Matthew 23:37 when Jesus said, "How often I have wanted to gather your children together as a hen protects her chicks beneath her wings." We are told in Isaiah 40:12 that God holds us in the hollow of his hand.

Loving the misshapen and needy is what God is all about. It's also what grace is all about. He sees me just as I am . . . missing tree branches and all. That's what is so compelling about the grace message. It's not about my looks or my performance. It's totally about God loving me and sending Jesus to die for my sin so that I am made into a masterpiece.

I love the explanation for how I could go from a misshapen tree to masterpiece. Remember with me this great verse in Ephesians 2:10: "For we are God's masterpiece. He has created us anew in Christ Jesus" (NLT). We become God's masterpiece the minute we receive Jesus as Savior. From that moment on, God sees not our imperfections but the perfection of Jesus, who lives within us.

That might make sense to us for a moment, but when we blow it . . . when we sin . . . when we behave like we did before we became a masterpiece, what does God see then? Romans 5:1 says, "Since we have been made right in God's sight by faith, we have peace with God because of what Jesus Christ our Lord has done for us" (NLT). According to this verse, what is in God's sight? We who have been made right, we who because of Jesus have become God's masterpiece.

It almost sounds too good to be true, doesn't it? We became a masterpiece because of Jesus. God then sees us as perfect. Yet the nagging question remains: what happens when I blow it? Can God's gracious love run out? Will he ultimately no longer see Jesus in me but instead see all my missing branches? Surely that day is coming sooner or later, isn't it? When it comes, what do I do?

Let's take a side trip back to the Old Testament. Do you remember the story of David, the king of Israel? David was a young shepherd tending to his sheep when God began setting him up to leave the pasture for a palace. History tells us David was a brilliant leader, one who loved God and faithfully honored him.

You may remember David was strolling the rooftop of his palace one afternoon when he saw a beautiful woman bathing on her own rooftop. Lust took over. David knew better. Nevertheless, he inquired about her and learned her name was Bathsheba. She was married to Uriah, who was one of David's band of "mighty men" (2 Samuel 23:39). That Bathsheba was married to one of his most loyal military leaders did not prevent David from sending for her.

Not only did David commit adultery, but he used his authority as king to have Uriah repositioned in the army so that battle circumstances would assure his death. When Uriah died in combat, David was guilty of not only adultery but murder. This behavior would be more understandable if it came from a pagan, but it came from one who loved and revered God.

How could David so blatantly go against all he believed and had given his life to? How did he manage the feelings of guilt and realization of the depths to which he had fallen? Psalm 32 describes his misery:

When I refused to confess my sin,
>   my body wasted away
>   and I groaned all day long.
> Day and night your hand of discipline was heavy on me.
>   My strength evaporated like water in the summer heat.
> Finally, I confessed all my sins to you
>   and stopped trying to hide my guilt.
> I said to myself, "I will confess my rebellion to the LORD."
>   And you forgave me! All my guilt is gone. (vv. 3–5 NLT)

What happens when God's people blow it? They (we) are like David—miserable. In fact, no one is more miserable than a sinning Christian. It's a little like walking with sharp stones in your shoes. Every step is worse than the last until finally your socks are bloody.

Some of us look for a cubby where we can hide and hope not to be discovered. We make a deal with Pugsy and ask her to move over and share her little plaid cushion until we at least stop bleeding. But that doesn't work either. There is only one solution for the believer who has sinned and run, or sinned and hidden, or sinned and gone into denial. We have to make our way out from behind the misshapen branches and show ourselves to God.

God has a very basic principle for his creation. We must first face what we have done that is wrong. In "shrink" jargon, we have to take ownership of our behavior. "I did it!" Once we admit and face our wrong, God says, "Tell me about it." That's what confession is—it's telling God what he already knows, but we have to have the experience of telling God. Then, and only then, God says, "I forgive you."

David, a believer in God, is a witness to us of how God's love does not run out or his grace run dry. When we sin, we hurt God. When we sin, we hurt ourselves. But the story does not have to end there. We have a choice to remain in our sin and be miserable or to confess our sin and be forgiven. We have a choice to hide behind the branches of a misshapen tree or to crawl out and rest in the shelter of God's eternal love.

David describes his choice at the conclusion of his Psalm 32 confession:

> For you are my hiding place;
>    you protect me from trouble.
> You surround me with songs of victory. (v. 7 NLT)

That, dear ones, is grace.

✻ ✻ ✻

*God, you are my hiding place. Whenever I am scared or lonely or in trouble, I will choose to curl up in the hollow of your hand and rest in your sheltering, eternal grace. Amen.*

# 35

# Grace Greater Than Our Sin

~ Nicole Johnson ~

Moreover the law entered that the offense might abound.
But where sin abounded, grace abounded much more.

—Romans 5:20 NKJV

In 1911, Julia Johnston and Daniel Towner penned the hymn "Grace Greater Than Our Sin." The theology is strong, and the words are so meaningful (and important) about grace.

> *Marvelous grace of our loving Lord,*
> *Grace that exceeds our sin and our guilt!*
> *Yonder on Calvary's mount outpoured*
> *There where the blood of the lamb was spilt.*

This hymn makes a pretty bold claim: *grace exceeds our sin and our guilt!*

To exceed is to go beyond the limits of something in quantity, degree, or scope. Is there truly more grace than sin? Is grace deeper and wider than all the sin in the world? Before you just answer yes (from your head), think for a moment about your own life. Have you ever put your sin up against God's grace? Did the grace win, or did the sin keep you from the grace?

Martin Luther wrote that we reveal what we truly believe about Christ by what we do in response to our own sin. Do we really believe that his grace exceeds our sin and our guilt? Or do we walk about feeling sinful and guilty most of the time?

*Grace, grace, God's grace,*
*Grace that will pardon and cleanse within;*
*Grace, grace, God's grace,*
*Grace that is greater than all our sin.*

Many people never acknowledge the depth of their sin. Others fall into a different trap, making too much of their sin and allowing it to separate them from God.

"I've done too much."

"I've gone too far."

"If you knew what I've done . . ."

Even though we have a Savior, how often do we try to manage sin ourselves? We act like it is no big deal and sweep it under the rug, or we try to do enough good works to offset it in our minds. In essence, we become sin managers rather than followers of Christ who made provision for our sin.

But we cannot outsin God's grace. His grace is greater.

Those aren't my words; they were written by the apostle Paul: "Where sin abounded, grace abounded much more" (Romans 5:20 NKJV). It's an extremely bold claim that only the gospel of Jesus Christ offers.

> Dark is the stain that we cannot hide.
> What can avail to wash it away?
> Look! There is flowing a crimson tide,
> Brighter than snow you may be today.

I am a spiller. My clothes are marked with coffee, tomato sauce, ink, and grease spots. Just the other day I was telling myself to be careful stirring the tomato sauce because I was wearing a white blouse and I didn't want to ruin it. But when I looked down to see how I was doing, I saw about ten tiny spots from the boiling bubbles that had splattered my blouse. It certainly was a stain that I could not hide.

Sin is a dark stain, the hymn says. We can't hide it very well. What if we wore our souls like T-shirts? What would the stains look like? What would avail to wash them away? Not our favorite box of laundry detergent, only the red crimson tide of his blood, shed for us out of the complete and unmerited favor of God. Just his grace—grace that is greater, stronger, more powerful than all our sin.

What would it mean to fully acknowledge our sin? What if we kept an honest account of all the things that we do that go contrary to God and his ways—things we do intentionally and things we do unintentionally? The list would certainly be long, too long in fact to keep accurately on any given day, much less for any length of time. But doesn't it make sense that the more fully we acknowledge our sin, the more fully we are humbled by his grace?

Jesus said as much. In Luke 7:36–43, we read of Jesus' encounter with Simon, the Pharisee. A woman has come to pour oil on Jesus' feet. Simon the Pharisee is pretty much appalled. Jesus asks Simon a question and paints a picture for him of two men. One has been forgiven a lot of money, and one has been forgiven a little. Then he asks Simon, "Who do you think loves more?" Simon replies, "The man who has been forgiven the most."

Jesus says, "You have answered correctly." Christ reveals that we love in accordance with (or in response to) the forgiveness (the grace) that we have been shown.

Forgiveness is forgiveness, you might say. A little or a lot—it's really all the same, right? If we miss the mark, it doesn't matter if we miss it by an inch or by a mile. While this is true from God's perspective, Jesus is tackling our perspective in his interaction with Simon. He is challenging our view of our own sin. Do we think we only need a little of God's grace because we just missed it by an inch? We were almost good enough to hit the mark on our own and we just needed a little of God's grace to cover our sin?

Jesus said this thinking affects the way we love God more than anything else.

James 4:6 tells us that God resists the proud but gives grace to the humble. Who are the humble but those who know how great their sin is? Who are the proud but those who think they don't sin as much as others?

*Marvelous, infinite, matchless grace,*
*Freely bestowed on all who believe!*
*You that are longing to see His face,*
*Will you this moment His grace receive?*

Regarding God's marvelous grace, Charles Spurgeon writes, "Who has ever returned from His door unblessed? Who has ever risen from His table unsatisfied, or from his bosom un-emparadised? His mercies are new every morning and fresh every evening. Who can know the number of his benefits or recount the list of His bounties? Every sand which drops from the glass of time is but the tardy follower of a myriad of mercies."[13]

This is the matchless grace that is freely bestowed upon us . . . grace that is greater.

✢ ✢ ✢

*Father, how can we thank you enough for the grace that you give? How can our hearts or our lips fully express the gratitude that we have for your goodness and mercy? Out of your infinite riches comes infinite grace and how blessed we are to receive it. We give all we can, out of our poverty, and you without limits, give and give again. Teach us to recognize how great your grace is, and to trust that it is greater than all our sin. Thank you, and thank you. Amen.*

# 36

# Marker Moments

~ Carol Kent ~

For the wages of sin is death, but the free gift of God is eternal life through Christ Jesus our Lord.

—Romans 6:23 NLT

My assistant, Shirley, was breathless. Her words were staggering: "Quick. Turn on the television. A plane just crashed into the World Trade Center in New York City!"

I was still groggy following a weekend ministry trip and a long flight home. Within minutes after I had turned on the TV, the cameras showed another plane hitting the second tower. That experience, combined with the rest of the tragic events of that day, is indelibly etched in my mind. And now, years later, September 11, 2001 has become "a marker moment" for all of us.

Marker moments are those times when something happens that is so significant it forever changes our future. Some marker moments are remembered with great joy, such as falling in love, getting married, celebrating the birth of a child, earning a diploma, being promoted to a long-sought position, receiving a large financial blessing, or coming to know Christ.

Other marker moments are not so pleasant, such as when your spouse announces the marriage is over, when your boss tells you the company is downsizing, when the pregnancy test is negative again, when you receive a phone call with news that your child has been arrested, or when the doctor says that you or a loved one has a terminal illness.

One of life's unexpected blessings is that difficult marker moments often become the springboard for a positive choice that makes its own significant impression on our lives.

In the weeks after 9/11, the United States was still reeling with uncertainty and fear. Airport security was tighter, our borders were more secure, and major sporting events insisted on fans entering through metal detectors as part of the precautions taken to ensure safety. It was a time of anxiety for people who traveled by air, as all of us who make our livelihood by flying to distant locations had to get back on an airplane in less than a week following the deadliest terrorist attack the United States has ever experienced.

In October 2001, I was scheduled to speak at a women's conference in Oahu, Hawaii. My husband, Gene, and I had been looking forward to this trip for a long time and had already decided to take a few extra vacation days following the event so we could enjoy the exquisite beaches, explore the tropical vegetation of the windward side of the island where there were fewer tourists, and take a day to visit the Polynesian Village. But following such catastrophic events in the continental US, the seeming dangers of going on this trip diminished our enthusiasm tremendously.

So much planning had already gone into this event that the conference committee definitely wanted to move forward with plans to host the event. Women from the surrounding islands of Kauai, Maui, and the "Big Island" (Hawaii) had already purchased their tickets, and the registration count was excellent. With mixed emotions we boarded our plane, stopping briefly in Seattle before landing at the airport on Oahu, the most populated of the Hawaiian Islands.

Hawaii provided everything the brochures promised—warm, tropical breezes, glorious sunsets, lush rain forests, and the irresistible combination of sandy beaches, blue seas, and perfect weather on multiple coastlines. Once we arrived in this tropical paradise, any fear of flying quickly dissipated.

The women's conference was an extraordinary joy as native Hawaiians joined newer residents and a good number of tourists to sing praise and worship while hula dancers used their remarkable gifts to bring God glory. Several of the participants made first-time commitments to Christ, and God's Spirit was powerful during the event. For many women, the "marker moment" of beginning a walk of faith with Jesus as their personal Savior was the highlight of the weekend.

I had agreed to speak at two worship services on the

Sunday following the women's conference. We arrived early, and I enjoyed observing the casual and comfortable open-air church. There was a roof, but the walls had openings that allowed the cool, tropical breezes to provide natural air-conditioning. When the service began, I once again appreciated the powerful way the native Hawaiians blended their music into a rich and moving chorus of praise to the One who created their beautiful island.

During a coffee break following the first service, an attractive young woman approached me. "Do you have time to talk?" she asked hesitantly.

"Yes, I'd love to get better acquainted. Let's take our coffee cups over to this bench where we'll have a little privacy," I said, moving in the direction of a less congested area.

Her face was lovely, but I could sense a deep cloud of sadness over her countenance. "My name is Stacey," she began. "I am a United Airlines flight attendant, and I have lived in Boston for the last couple of years because that's the city where I embark on most of my assigned trips." I could see tears forming in the corners of her eyes. She continued, "One of my regular flights was one of the planes that crashed into the World Trade Center—but September 11 was my day off that week. Another flight attendant died in my place."

Neither of us could speak for a moment. With the tragedy happening so recently, it was overwhelming to think of how close she had come to death. I offered a few words of comfort, and then she continued, "I have been so afraid that I took an indefinite leave from my job and came home to my native Hawaii. I'm trying to find an answer to my fear, and I'm trying to find God. Can you help me?"

"Oh, yes. I can help you!" I responded.

I have rarely met anyone who so desperately wanted to accept Christ and know that her sins were forgiven and that she would have heaven as her final destination if she put her faith and trust in Him. I briefly recounted the simple gospel message: "God loves you, and he sent his son, Jesus, to this earth to live a perfect and sinless life. Religious leaders of the day mocked Jesus and eventually crucified him. When he died, he paid the price for your sins and mine. But the best part of the story is that Jesus rose again, and today he is in heaven preparing a place for everyone who believes."

Stacey listened attentively. I continued, "There's a wonderful verse in the Bible I'd like to read to you: 'For the wages of sin is death, but the free gift of God is eternal life through Christ Jesus our Lord' (Romans 6:23 NLT) .Would you like to ask Jesus into your life right now?"

"Yes," Stacey responded emphatically. "I don't want to live in fear anymore. I want to know that if I die—whether it's on a plane or in another way—I will live forever in heaven when I leave this earth."

That day, on a little white bench on the grounds of a tiny church on the island of Oahu, Stacey had the most important "marker moment" of her life. She bowed her head and invited Jesus to be her Savior and Lord. Looking up, with a radiant expression, she said, "Thank you. I'm giving my fear to God. Thank you for leading me to him."

✽ ✽ ✽

*Father, thank you that the most significant marker moment of our lives is when we give you our fears, our past mistakes, our bad choices, and our anxiety and ask for a brand-new beginning. Thank you for sending your son to die on the cross for us so we can have hope and confidence that we will live with you in heaven for eternity. Amen.*

# 37

# Grace in Sickness and Death

## ~ Thelma Wells ~

For the grace of God that brings salvation has appeared to all men, teaching us that, denying ungodliness and worldly lusts, we should live soberly, righteously, and godly in the present age, looking for the blessed hope and glorious appearing of our great God and Savior Jesus Christ.

—Titus 2:11–13 NKJV

Rettie was a petite package of intelligence, creativity, and talent. A soloist whose voice on a bad day was more remarkable than a robin redbreast chirping praises to God. With her head held high, her posture straight, her hands clasped together in front of her waist, her eyes focused on God, and her mouth singing with precision and perfect tonal quality "Ave Maria" or "The Lord's Prayer," her music would bring tears to the listeners' eyes as she praised the God of the universe in song.

The only time I witnessed Rettie's inability to reach the highest note in an aria was a few weeks before her passing.

Even then she had perfect stance and poise. I think she knew it was her last solo, so she was determined to sing one of her favorite songs, "Ride On, King Jesus." When she got near the end of the song and was singing "Ride on, ride on . . ." her physical weakness caused her to be unable to make those notes, but she was not bothered by that imperfection. She continued to sing until the last note was finished. She took a slow, unsteady bow and was helped back to her seat on the podium. I thought then that this was Reetie's finale.

In the more than sixty years that I knew Reetie, she was always different from what you called an average girl. She spoke with proper grammar. She dressed like she stepped off the page of the most prestigious fashion magazine. She decorated her home with style and warm comfort. Her husband and son enjoyed the sweetness and freedom of amusement, great gourmet cooking, dinner parties, fabulous vacations, social and community involvement, and church work together as a family. I was a part of her extended family along with a group of ladies who grew up in the church together, from nursery school through college. Reetie and I enjoyed the fact that she and I dated during the same time, got married near the same time, and were pregnant around the same time. Her son and one of my daughters, Lesa, went to the senior prom together. I had the opportunity to know Reetie up close and personal.

One of our most enjoyed social outlets was when we would get together with the ladies we grew up with in our church, St. John Missionary Baptist Church in Dallas, Texas. We call ourselves "The Committee." No, we're not organized at all. This name came from the first person in our committee to go home to be with the Lord, Beverly. On one of the occasions we got together to just have fun, her husband asked where she was going. Ms. Quick Tongue Bev said, "To a committee meeting with T. Wells and the girls." When she got there, we all had a big laugh about the "committee meeting" and began then to call ourselves "The Committee." There were eight of us in this group of ladies who all had nicknames: Kat, BB, Betty K, Baby Derl, Gwennie, Marget, T. Wells, Dr. Harris. B. Walls, and Reetie. We were such great friends that one could not hurt without the other feeling some of the pain. All of our mothers were each other's mother, too. And all of us had one significant thing in common: we came to salvation in Jesus as very young girls not because we were so good or smart (even though we were smart and all had college degrees), but because the grace of God was shed abroad in our hearts and we accepted this free gift of the salvation of Jesus and allowed him to work in our hearts for more than four decades.

What the point of my telling you all that? Reetie was diagnosed with cancer a number of months before I was. When she got the news and shared it with us, there was no fear in her voice, no challenge in her demeanor, no anxiety in her voice, no pessimism in her perception of what she was facing. The months of chemotherapy and radiation treatments, loss of hair, weakened body, diminishing quality of life, and what began to look hopeless to us and her family were illuminated by her never-say-die attitude. Every time you'd see or talk to Reetie, she would brighten your day by responding to "How do you feel?" with something uplifting or encouraging, like, "God is good girl; he's in control" or "I'm feeling nicely today, thank the Lord" or "I'm happy to see you, girl."

This kind of pleasantness continued through three years of fighting this dread disease. Yes, even the last week of her life while she still had energy to answer that never-ending question about how she felt, she would say something like, "I could feel better, but it's going to be just fine. I'm in God's hands, and Jesus is taking care of me."

In the final days of her earthly life when her only nephew, Dr. Frederick Douglas Haines III, pastor of the Friendship West Baptist Church in Dallas, asked her how she felt just before she became too sick to talk, Reetie's response was, "I'm just trying to make God look good." And without a doubt, Reetie, you did make God look good by your life, your ways, and your support, but mostly by accepting his saving power freely given to you by the grace of God. All the good you did could not merit that grace or sustain that grace. It was a gracious gift of love given by the Master of love, bestowed by the Son of love, Jesus the Christ, the Son of the living God.

Watching someone like Reetie go through pain with such poise was cause for reflection. How could she still be so proper? When Reetie encouraged you rather than you encouraging her, you would wonder how she could be so positive. When she greeted you with such welcome arms and delight as she lay on her sickbed, you couldn't help but wonder: if you were in the same place for the same reason experiencing the agony of pain as she was, could you have the same power to create life in a dying place? Was it God's grace that gave her this ability? Or was it her acceptance of Jesus the Savior that gave her the grit to suffer long and maintain her self-control? Yes!

I believe that God's redeeming grace gives us the ability to make it through the hardest times in life with the dignity of God, the power of Jesus, and the comfort of the Holy Spirit. When Reetie accepted the grace of God and was saved to new life in him, this opened the door for all the mercies and fruits of the Spirit to rule and reign in her mortal body so when this earthy body is no more, she will live with him in the heavenlies for eternity, world without end.

It was by God's amazing grace that Reetie could stand before men and women and declare that her task was to make God look good because God had given her something she did not deserve, could not barter for, demand, crave, purchase, or take; all she would do was to accept it in her heart. This acceptance, in my feeble opinion, was the anchor of her ability to die with dignity because she knew that one of these days the grace of God would be made perfect in her life and she would finally understand the ambiguous unfathomed present of grace through faith in our Lord Jesus Christ. Accepting the grace of God helped Reetie make God look good.

Have you accepted this magnificent, indescribable free gift from God? It's really simple, so simple that many don't understand how easy it is. All you have to do is to confess with your mouth that you are a sinner by nature and that you believe that God raised Jesus from the dead. When you acknowledge that and ask Jesus, with all your heart, soul, and spirit, to come into your heart and live there, and commit to make him controller of your life, you then receive that free gift of salvation that very instant.

That's so painless that people miss the point. Grace is the free gift of unmerited favor. It's something you can't work for; God just gives it to you for the asking. He's like a good father. He wants to give you grace. Grace that is greater than all your needs. He gave it to Reetie and all The Committee, and he longs to give it to you!

✣ ✣ ✣

*Father, thank you for your unmerited grace toward us that helps us, when we receive this grace, live and die spending our lives making you look good so others will accept the benefits of your infinite grace. Amen.*

# 38

# Grace for Eternity

~ Sandi Patty ~

Therefore, as God's chosen people, holy and dearly loved
. . . Bear with each other and forgive whatever grievances
you may have against one another. Forgive as the Lord forgave you. And over all these virtues put on love, which
binds them all together in perfect unity.

—Colossians 3:12–14 NIV

It has been a never-ending struggle for me to accept God's
grace in my life. Grace is something I have no problem
singing about or telling others about, but when it comes to
telling myself about it, I seem to hit a brick wall. It's even
easy sometimes for me to extend grace to another person,
but to receive it, either from God or someone else, is something that I often have a hard time doing.

I have been blessed for the last thirteen years to be a stepmother to three amazing kids—Donnie, Aly, and Mollie
Peslis. Being a stepparent, for those of you who know, is a
wonderfully challenging experience. My husband, Don, and

I tried in the beginning of our blendedness to treat each kid as equal and the same. However, we quickly realized this was much easier said than done. When I would speak to my own children—Anna, Jon, Jenn, and Erin—I could say something like, "Hey, knock it off" or "Keep your hands to yourself," and I could say it in a rough and tough "mom" voice. However, when I would attempt that with my stepchildren, I truly came across as the wicked stepmother. That is a role I would rather not play. We quickly realized that Don needed to be the heavy with his kids and I needed to be the heavy with my kids. A stepparent is much like the role a beloved teacher or mentor might play in a child's life. Important, encouraging yet with different boundaries as a parent. All that to say, I have been so very blessed to be a stepmom to some pretty wonderful kids.

I have also been blessed to share the raising of these kids with Don and his former spouse, Michelle. Early on, Don and Michelle developed an easygoing, work-together relationship. They never had a set schedule of visitation like many divorced parents do. They just kind of made it up as they went and listened carefully to the kids. It was truly amazing for me to watch. Early on, Michelle decided that what was best for the kids was what she wanted to focus on, and she and Don and I were able to put our adult issues aside. I appreciated that in her so much. And I have been so privileged to share in the child rearing with her.

In early January 2007, I watched my three beautiful stepchildren grieve the passing of their mother, Michelle. Michelle had been valiantly battling cancer for more than seven years. Her cancer went from breast, to lymph, to bone, to brain, to liver, to lungs . . . something that honestly is very hard for me to even fathom. Each time she would battle through with chemo and the love of her family. And each time, after a short period of remission, the cancer would return. And she would once again battle. In December 2006, it became clear that her days of battling were coming to an end.

Michelle is someone to whom I caused great pain. When my relationship with Don (my husband) began, Don was still married to Michelle, and I was also married to someone else. My choices caused so many people hurt, but especially Michelle. And as I watched her battle cancer the last seven years of her life, my guilt and shame became so burdensome to me.

But many years ago, Michelle offered me something that seemed unthinkable for me to take. She offered me grace and forgiveness. She and I began to work well together on behalf of the children. She told me she wasn't concerned whether I accepted her grace, but for her to move on with her life, she said she needed to offer it. And I needed to try to accept it. She modeled for me that forgiving someone doesn't necessarily change the other person, but it frees you. Michelle forgave me because that is what she needed for her healing.

And then she got cancer. I know life isn't fair, but that seemed so unjust! And she battled. I truly believe that she lived as long as she did because she wasn't carrying around hurt and bitterness. She decided to let those things go, and she lived . . . offering grace and forgiveness so that I might live as well. And she modeled for her children how to move through their own pain with grace and dignity.

When God decided it was time to take Michelle home, she quietly passed on into the next life . . . the eternal life that we all long for. She was in her home in Michigan surrounded by her new husband—she remarried after she and Don divorced—and her children. Don was there as well because he was part of her story and the story of their kids.

My children and I were home in Indiana sharing this with them by phone, getting updates from Don so we would know what was going on. I will never forget all of us sitting in the kitchen at 1:30 a.m. and hearing that Michelle had passed on into eternity. We grieved for so many reasons. We mostly grieved for those we loved who were left behind and who were missing her so much.

We decided that when morning came we would go to Michigan to be with them, but needless to say none of us slept much that night. I lit candles in my room and turned on some beautiful meditative music. As I thought of Michelle, I began to cry, but not at this moment from sorrow. I realized in the quietness of my room that she had given me the greatest gift, besides Jesus, that anyone has ever given me. When she didn't have to, she offered me forgiveness. When it would have been understandable for her to turn her back on me, she offered me grace. And because she did, there was a sense of peace that came over me that would not have otherwise. But things were not left unspoken, and words were not left unsaid, and mercy was not left unleashed.

Michelle, as she danced her way into eternity, gave me a glimpse of the eternal in my heart. She taught me that letting go of the pain of our lives opens up a greater capacity in our soul to feel the eternal in our days. And because she did, I am learning to offer grace and forgiveness to myself. That, my friends, is the more challenging journey.

✳ ✳ ✳

*Lord, I need your strength and grace to forgive those who have hurt me. And when I have made choices that have hurt others, help me to humbly accept their forgiveness— and then give me the grace to forgive myself. Amen.*

# 39

# Mutual Grace

~ Luci Swindoll ~

Stay calm; mind your own business; do your own job. You've heard all this from us before, but a reminder never hurts. We want you living in a way that will command the respect of outsiders.

—1 Thessalonians 4:11–12 MSG

My mother would have been one hundred years old today—April 20, 2007. She died thirty-seven years ago at the age of sixty-three, long before her time. I'm already eleven years older than Mother when she passed away in 1971.

For many years, I'm sure I was a disappointment to mother in terms of my choices and lifestyle. As her only daughter, she wanted me to marry and have children, and I can't remember ever wanting to marry. She wanted me to be a home-maker, but getting a college degree was far more desirable to me than "making a home." *If* I went to college, Mother preferred that I major in home economics, yet I chose art and education. Mother said it was OK to sing in a church choir ("and that's enough"), but singing professionally in the Dallas Opera became one of the greatest thrills of my life. She would have been content for me never to leave the shores of America, but I wanted to travel all over the world experience other cultures, and learn other languages. To put it mildly, my mother and I were as different as daylight and dark.

But the one thing in which we were exactly alike was our love for God.

Having been reared in a Christian home, my mother knew a lot about the Ten Commandments, the Beatitudes, the Lord's Prayer, and the Gospels . . . but she knew very little about the truth of God's grace. She loved God and wanted to please him, but it more or less ended there. Thus, when her three children came along, those were the same teachings she emphasized and passed on to us. We all went to church together, but during those years we never learned more than the basics of salvation. And here's what's sad . . . we didn't know there was more. We just went with the flow of fundamental Christian principles, thinking that was enough. We never learned Hebrews 6:3: "But there's so much more. Let's get on with it!" (MSG). (I'm not sure we even knew there was a Hebrews 6:3!)

About this time, it was no longer a difference in choices that caused heartache between Mother and me; we hit major roadblocks. As we kids faced our teenage years with the typical problems and challenges and misunderstandings with parents, my older brother began going to a nondenominational church and invited us to join him for weeknight Bible studies. First, Mother and Daddy went, and then one by one, everybody in the family started attending. For the first time in our lives, we were being taught the basic doctrines of Scripture and how they could be applied.

Gradually, everything in our household changed . . . for the better. In that church, we found a fellowship of grace-oriented believers with whom we could share our hurts and questions. We found a teacher who was seminary trained and taught biblical doctrines that set us free from performance or rules. We found a biblical way through our various dilemmas and misunderstandings.

In short, we learned about God's infinite grace. And that changed everything. For everyone.

About this time, I remember giving my mother a Bible for her birthday. It was from my father and me. In the front, we wrote these words, *"He careth for you" (1 Peter 5:7) . . . and so do we!*

Now that Mother is gone, I have that Bible in my library. The other day, I was looking through it, reading her handwritten notes in the margins. One read, "Where there is a realization of grace, there will be no personality conflicts."

I have no idea when my mother wrote that, but I remember well the personality conflicts we had prior to her learning about the grace of God. While we were both enmeshed in rules, performance, and trying to get along with each other when it was so hard, nothing worked. But as Mother realized the place of grace in her life, I experienced a definite change in her behavior toward me. And the same was true of me. I found when my mother turned me over to God for reproof, guidance, and direction (instead of her own), I wanted to please her more. I didn't want to hurt her; I wanted to honor her. Once she left me alone, I felt closer to her and knew that things were changing for the better between us.

When a realization of grace enters a life, things start to happen in the affirmative. No one tries to boss somebody else around. No one makes another life her project. No one requires a certain performance level before she's accepted. There is love and understanding and patience. I began to see all these things in my mother, and I hoped she was seeing them in me because I, too, was being convicted about my judgmental spirit toward her. The more she let God direct me, the more I let go of my determination to have my way, no matter if it hurt her.

Instead of going to the homes of friends on school holidays, I wanted to go to my own home. I wanted to be with Mother. I longed to please her and hear her heart. I can tell you for a fact, this definitely would not have happened had infinite grace not entered both our hearts. We may have been very, very different in our hopes and dreams for the other, but when it came to grace in our lives, we wanted exactly the same thing.

It takes a long time to come to that place in a relationship. And so often, it's grace that smoothes the rough places between a mother and daughter. I've talked with countless friends and acquaintances who went through exactly the same thing with their mothers as I did with mine. They felt frustrated, manipulated, tired, angry, and ready to give up the whole idea of trying to get along. They've said to me, "It's not working. I want to run away." And I know exactly how they felt because it was what I had felt for years.

I wish it didn't take so long to learn how to accept people as they are. Some of us never learn, and that's unfortunate because we can't change each other. We can't make others behave or grow up into responsible adults. All we can do is model what Christ taught and work on tolerance and forgiveness in our own life.

Giving grace takes a lot of practice. By my behavior though, I want to be a reminder that it works. First Thessalonians 4:11–12 says, "Stay calm; mind your own business; do your own job. You've heard all this from us before, but a reminder never hurts. We want you living in a way that will command the respect of outsiders" (MSG).

And by the way, by the time my mother died, we had become very close friends. We enjoyed sweet fellowship and conversation on a daily basis. She often visited me in my home and had dinner at my table. Mother came to hear me sing in the opera every year and repeatedly told me how proud she was of me and what I had done with my life.

My mother had experienced the life-transforming, eternal grace of God—and it made all the difference.

✼ ✼ ✼

*God, help me accept people as they are and not try to change them into what I want them to be. And please give me the grace to extend the tolerance and forgiveness of Christ to others. Amen.*

# 40

# Grasp This Moment!

~ Sheila Walsh ~

One of the criminals hanging alongside cursed him: "Some Messiah you are! Save yourself! Save us!" But the other one made him shut up: "Have you no fear of God? You're getting the same as him. We deserve this, but not him—he did nothing to deserve this." Then he said, "Jesus, remember me when you enter your kingdom." He said, "Don't worry, I will. Today you will join me in paradise."

—Luke 23:39–43 MSG

We don't know anything about the life of the man on the cross next to Jesus that would give us a clear picture of him. We know he was a criminal bound for execution, and that's about it. But perhaps we can read between the lines a little. He was not like the other criminal being executed that day. The other prisoner was callous, hardened by life, and merciless. He joined the Roman soldiers in taunting Jesus.

They say that when you know you are in your last hours of life even the most heartless among us begin to wonder, *Is this all? Was my life for nothing? Is there really a God?* These somber, penitent thoughts seemed far removed from the soul of one so close to death. The prisoner suspended on the other side of Christ was outraged. "Have you no fear of God? . . . We deserve this, but not him—he did nothing to deserve this" (Luke 23:40–41 MSG).

How did he know that Jesus was innocent? Perhaps he had been part of the crowd one day and listened as Jesus talked. He may have sat on a hillside and been fed from a child's lunch through the hands of this most unusual man. If he was there, if he sensed that this man was different than any he had ever heard before, why did he end up being crucified beside him? He may have been arrested for a crime he had committed earlier and so for him, the truth came too late. Or perhaps he listened to Jesus offer hope and healing and for a moment began to believe that he could live a better life, but as he lay in bed at night he thought himself a fool to believe he could change his ways now. He had made too many poor choices, walked through too many wrong doors, and now life as it inevitably does had caught up with him.

But whatever his thoughts were, he was not going to let a common criminal berate the innocent man hanging between them. He turned his face toward the cross that held Jesus up for all to mock, and he made his last request on this earth, "Jesus, remember me when you enter your kingdom" (Luke 23:42 MSG). Whatever wrong choices this man had made in life, with his final breaths he made the only choice that eternally matters. He saw beyond another prisoner being executed to Messiah, King of kings. He asked for the grace that would be eternal. Jesus heard not just his words but his heart and answered his cry: "Today you will join me in paradise" (v. 43 MSG).

The word Jesus used for *Paradise* in this verse is the same word used to describe the *Garden of Eden*. When you reflect on the grace offered to this man in the last hours of his life, it is remarkable. Jesus tells him that the life once tasted by Adam and Eve will be his as well. His past may be filled with the fruit of the Fall, but his future will be the marriage feast of the Lamb.

When we speak of grace, we define it as unmerited favor; and yet so often we feel as if somehow we should measure up to this gift. In the life of the man on the third cross, grace becomes abundantly clear. There is not one thing he can do now to live a life worthy of the call other than open his heart to the love of God. There is not one deed he can do as a last-minute, "Thank you!" All he can do is accept Jesus' gift. That is grace.

For some of us, grace is a disturbing gift. It's disturbing because it is no respecter of persons. Imagine that the man on the third cross had a brother. This brother lived a life of total devotion to God; he sacrificed his heart and his life and his money to honor God in every way he knew possible. His path finally led him to the foot of the cross, where he recognized the Lamb of God and called out for mercy. The grace that would be extended to him would be the same as to the brother who had wasted his life. "That doesn't seem fair," you might say. I would agree with you— it's not fair; it's grace.

Jesus told a story in Matthew 20:1–16 to illustrate how hard this can be for the human heart to make peace with. All of Jesus' parables began with elements that would be familiar to his audience, but they often took a disturbing turn.

He asked the crowd to imagine a man going out in the first light of day to hire workers for his fields. A normal day then was twelve hours counting breaks, usually beginning at about 6 a.m. The man told those he hired that he would pay them a denarius, which was the going rate for a day worker or soldier. At 9 a.m., he went out and hired a few more hands and also at noon. In the last hour of the working day, at 5 p.m., he saw some men standing around in the marketplace doing nothing. When he asked them why, they told him that no one had hired them all day, so he put them to work for that last hour. Then he asked his foreman to pay all the day laborers. It would have been customary to pay the ones who had worked longest, but the foreman had been instructed to pay those last in before the others.

This sets up the whole point of Jesus' story. If those who worked longest had been paid first, they could have taken their pay and left, but that would have negated the lesson on grace. When the workers who had been there all day saw that the men who had only worked an hour were paid a denarius, I'm sure they were thrilled. *If these guys got that much for an hour, can you imagine how much we'll get!*

There were high-fives all over the field until those who had worked all day received their pay. It was exactly the same amount as those who had worked for only sixty minutes. They were furious. The landowner told them that he paid them exactly what he told them he would. He had not short-changed them in any way. He asked, "Don't I have the right to do what I want with my own money? Or are you envious because I am generous?" (v. 15 NIV).

The grace of God is not about what seems fair to us. Heaven's eternal economy of grace is all about God's heart, not our hard work or good behavior.

Perhaps there is someone new in your circle, and you struggle a little with the path that has led this person to the freedom she now enjoys. Trust God's heart and celebrate with him the gift of eternal grace.

✽ ✽ ✽

*Father, I am so grateful that your grace isn't about getting what's fair! No matter what I do or how hard I try, I could never deserve your gift of salvation. Thank you for looking beyond what is fair and instead sending your Son to die in my place so that you could extend to me your gift of eternal grace. Amen.*

# In Memory of
# Barbara Johnson

Barbara Johnson was an amazing combination of tough and tender, heart and humor, laughter and tears. She gave comfort and challenge—sometimes in the same sentence. She made us laugh and cry, think and feel, look inside ourselves, and reach out to others. She was an enigma and an energizer. She gave herself and everything she owned to the God she loved and a cause she believed in. She rescued, befriended, and loved. She cared, and never more than when she sensed someone wasn't being cared for. She raised the bar high for what it meant to be the hands and feet of Jesus on planet earth. The homeless came home with her; the helpless found help; the hurting were healed; and the heartless were on dangerous ground with Barbara.

She's impossible to explain or understand and impossible not to love. That's why when she was diagnosed with a brain tumor in 2001, our hearts were broken to learn she'd not be traveling with the Women of Faith team again. And when she fought the battle with that menacing brain tumor, she never lost her focus on reaching out to others. (When we visited her in the hospitals, she never greeted us in any other way than to say, "Did you bring me books I can give away? There are a lot of hurting people in here.") And when she lost that battle with cancer, she won the war of her life. She stepped into eternity where the streets are lined with people she's known and loved, helped, encouraged and healed.

We love you, Barbara Johnson, and are inspired by your courageous life. We dedicate this book to you. You gave infinite grace to all of us, especially when we needed it most.

# 41

# Barbara Johnson

~ Mary Graham ~

Barbara Johnson was a pistol—and I knew that the first day I met her. She was smart, spunky, and absolutely full of surprises. In 1996, she was the first woman Steve Arterburn phoned when he decided to create a ministry called the Joyful Journey, which later became Women of Faith. If there was going to be a journey full of joy, Steve knew Barbara had to be part of the package. She was famous for joy—and equally so for heartache.

Life dealt Barbara one difficult blow after another, but her response to all of it—the good, bad, and ugly—was effervescent joy. As she often said, "Pain is inevitable, but misery is optional." And it was one option she never exercised.

When our paths crossed in 1996, I was amused and bedazzled by her. She was the most unique character I have ever known . . . at one moment full of encouragement and in an instant, she would challenge you, your thinking, and your behavior to the core.

Always strong and independent, she could really be a team

player. She was full of courage and compassion, and encouraged others to be. In spite of facing crises, she maintained a sense of humor and a spirit of confidence in the sovereignty of God.

She was a master of the one-liner: "Life is tough, but God is faithful," "It's not over till it's over," and her famous, "Stick a geranium in your hat and be happy."

Her life was an open book; her pain freely broadcast to the world; her suffering never denied nor hidden away. She strongly believed if God could meet her in agony, he could and would meet anyone there. She felt no need to hide anything that might be an encouragement to someone else. Interestingly, she didn't hesitate to tell you what she herself had suffered, but her lips were sealed when it came to what she gave to those who suffered.

Like the time we were in Charlotte, North Carolina, for the weekend. On Saturday during the lunch break, someone on our staff came to tell me a story. Apparently, on Friday night after the event, one of the local TV stations featured the Women of Faith conference at the local arena. A woman, who said she was hiding from her pimp and sleeping in a Dumpster, saw the story on the TV in a bar. She saw the women in the audience singing and laughing, but what really struck her was watching Barbara Johnson address the audience. Barbara was wearing a campaign-type button (which she always wore) that said in large letters, "God loves somebody who has AIDS."

That button made the woman want to find Barbara. She made her way to the arena on Saturday, which was no small task since the Charlotte arena in those days was a long distance from downtown. When the woman finally arrived, we were all on a lunch break. Outside the arena, women were having box lunches on the lawn. She went up to a circle of friends and asked if they could take her to Barbara Johnson.

Seeing how desperate she was, someone in the group decided to give it a try, so she went to an usher, who found a staff member, who found someone backstage, who found me, and we all heard the story. Knowing Barbara as we did, it was no surprise to any of us that she'd be very eager to interrupt her lunch break to meet the woman in need. When they finally met face to face, Barbara immediately pinned the huge "God loves" button on her. Then we heard her whole story, which was painful and scary.

That's when Barbara set a plan in motion. First, she took us all to the locker room in the arena and asked the woman if she wanted to take a shower. When she said yes, she sent one of the Women of Faith staff upstairs to the concourse to get her a clean T-shirt (the only apparel we had!). She helped her bathe and washed her hair.

When the woman emerged from the shower, she realized Barbara had thrown away her very dirty shirt. She said, "Oh, but get the button. I want the button. I want it on my new shirt!"

By the time the program was back in session, Barb knew everything she needed to know about her new friend and she'd decided what to do. The woman had one relative she trusted in Chicago, and she knew she'd be safe there. Barbara got a cab to take the woman to the train station, gave her money for a one-way ticket to Chicago, gave her a big hug and sent her on her way . . . just after praying with her and sharing the gospel.

When she left, I said to Barbara, "What if she doesn't use the money to go to her grandmother's? What if her story isn't true?" Barbara looked at me with the softest eyes, and in the sweetest voice she said with such kindness, "What if her story is true, Mary? We'll never know. But we'll always know we helped her."

And that's why we all loved Barbara Johnson so dearly. It's why we called her every day, and then every week after her diagnosis. It's why we wanted to stay in constant touch. It's why even brain cancer didn't keep Barbara from reaching out to anyone in need and always finding a way to help. It's why every time we visited her, regardless of where she was or what her present condition was, her first words were, "Did you bring me some books to give away?"

One time I asked her if she was afraid to die. She laughed at me. "Oh, Mary," she said, "Of course not. I can't lose. I have loved ones in heaven I long to see. And loved ones here I long to be with. Whether I live or die, I can't lose, can I? I can't lose!"

Barbara Johnson gave her life away, and in spite of all her losses on this earth, she didn't lose. In the end, she gained life everlasting.

# 42

# Dear Barbara

~ Patsy Clairmont ~

Dear Barbara,

Are there geraniums in heaven?

I remember that despite the overwhelming response to your best-selling book *Stick a Geranium in Your Hat and Be Happy*, your favorite flowers were actually lilacs. So I guess I should be asking, are there lilacs crowding the doorsteps of your mansion? I enjoy picturing you knee-deep in their fragrant purple clusters, beaming with relief and awe to finally be with Jesus.

I've wondered with all the people you impacted on earth, was there a "great cloud of witnesses" waiting to greet you? Like your two darling sons who left you too soon for heaven's shore, your dear hubby Bill, your sweet sister Janet, and others you loved who got a jump-start on eternity . . . and now you're there with them.

Barb, we talked on a number of occasions about heaven, and I know you longed for it. We (your Porch Pals) didn't want you to leave us, but we understood why you wanted to. We realize we won't be far behind your footprints on his shore . . . and then we'll resume our friendships and a whole new way of enjoying Jesus together.

I wish you could send me a postcard and brief me on Jesus . . . as if he could be briefed. But you know what I mean: just give us a little peek behind the veil and of how he fills your every breath. Oh, and what does his voice sound like? Many waters? Thunder? A summer's breeze? A symphony? Probably all the above and more. Tell me about the light that emanates from Jesus; it must be dazzling to light all of eternity.

And, Barbara, what's the food like? You know how I love to eat. Any humus? I hear that's really healthy . . . but then healthy is a done deal there. I know how you and Bill made almost daily trips to In and Out for hamburgers when you were here; I bet you don't even miss them now that you're at the banqueting table.

Barbara, I know you are at perfect peace, but I wonder since there's no night, do you sleep in heaven? I remember your fondness for power naps. Are you still writing? I remember how you never went anywhere without a pen. Why you even drove your car with a ballpoint tucked securely between your fingers. Not to mention that you spoke onstage with a pen in your grip and more than once you jotted last-minute notes on the palm of your hand so you wouldn't forget something you wanted to tell your friends. And the audiences truly were your friends.

You were greatly loved. You stood tall in your losses and pain when others of lesser fiber would have stooped and shriveled. And you opened up your heart publicly and allowed God to redeem your greatest pain for his highest purposes and for the good of his people.

Everywhere we traveled for Women of Faith conferences, girlfriends from that city lined up to take you to dinner or to show you the city's sites. I saw their gratitude in their eyes and in their smiles. They loved you for offering them a rope of hope and for setting the costly example of what it means to press on.

And press on you did. You taught us that sorrow will touch us all and that Jesus is greater than any ploy of the enemy or any heartache we suffer. And then you demonstrated courage by the fun-loving way you lived. You loved to laugh, and you loved to cause others to giggle. You are the only friend I've known who devoted an entire room in your home to joy!

More than once I retrieved packages from my front porch with Spatula stickers on them. Inside you would include an outrageous gift for my husband: a hip-swinging singing frog or a roller-skating yodeling bear. One time it was a box with a voice inside yelling, "Let me out of here!" Always it was something that made us laugh. That seemed to be the calling on your life . . . spreading joy.

Remember the time I made a goof in a magazine article and you called me up to chat about it? We got so tickled over my innocent error that we almost needed oxygen to recover! I love that memory; it was so full of life-giving friendship endorphins.

Another phone call that was precious to me was after you had read my contributions to one of our devotionals and you wanted me to know how much you had enjoyed them. You definitely were a cheerleader. It was your norm to take time out of each day to call and applaud someone.

I loved seeing the trail of generosity you left everywhere you went. You were always doling out your books to hotel clerks, waitresses, limo drivers, and cleaning personnel, as well as providing scholarships for the conferences to those who couldn't afford to attend. I remember more than once when you footed the bill for burgers for our truck drivers and all our production crew. Often you brought speaking buddies your glitzy watches, earrings, and pins that sparkled with fun. And there's no way to add up the countless hours you spent on the telephone splashing joy on women with crushed spirits.

We still quote you at Women of Faith, and I'm sure we always will. You were the queen of quotes. You collected thousands of them from your many grateful fans and then liberally doused your books and talks with them in a desire to spread hope.

If I could highlight only one of your sterling contributions, it would have to be your courageous campaign to support families with gay children. When no one else would even broach the subject, you stepped in with candor and grace. You spoke of the redemptive power of love and the healing journey of reconciliation. And while you didn't minimize the shattering impact, you compassionately embraced every member of the distraught family . . . *every member*.

What a legacy you have left—a delightful friend, a bold advocate for the downtrodden, and a generous benefactress.

Keep the lilacs watered, girlfriend . . . we'll see you soon!

Love,
Patsy

# 43

# Barbara Johnson

~ Marilyn Meberg ~

It was seventeen years ago, but I well remember my experience. I was wandering around in a facility where I was to
attend a speakers' prayer meeting. I thought I knew where I
was going . . . but obviously I didn't. Each room I peeked
into was empty. The conference started in thirty minutes,
and I wasn't sure how to find that location either. I turned
the handle on yet another door and was relieved to see ten
women standing in a circle holding hands; someone was
praying aloud.

As I quietly crept toward the circle, an outstretched hand
reached for me and pulled me in. She squeezed my hand as if
to say, "You're okay . . . you've come to the right place." I
sneaked a quick look at my benefactor and in a flash of recognition said to myself, *Oh my . . . that's Barbara Johnson!* She
caught my sneak look and returned it with a wink. I loved her
immediately.

Barbara and I had never met before, but I was certainly
aware of her. I knew she inspired laughter in people who

thought their personal pain would never permit laughter again. I knew she inspired people to maintain their faith in a loving God despite circumstances that looked unloving. I knew she inspired people to love their kids in spite of the choices they made. I knew she dared to talk about a subject rarely discussed publicly in the Christian community. Through the anguish of her own experience with her son, Barbara gave a voice to those who had no words . . . to those parents too confused and ashamed to acknowledge their child was struggling with a same-sex preference. She helped those parents say the word . . . *homosexual*. She helped them to choose love instead of judgment and rejection. This monumental task was accomplished because Barbara dared to tell her own story. I had heard her story but had not personally experienced her heart until that morning in the prayer circle.

As I got to know Barbara through the years, I realized it was second nature for her to reach out to people who weren't sure where they were going. It was second nature for her to pull people into her circle, squeeze their hand, and give them a wink of assurance. Barbara's heart was huge, and her generosity knew no limits.

One of my favorite examples of Barbara's gracious heart as well as zany humor occurred in her hometown of La Habra, California. She had walked into the city police station to personally pay a speeding ticket she had received the day before. Incidentally, one of the many things Barbara and I had in common was exceeding the posted speed limit. Neither of us felt we were wild or reckless, just in a hurry.

All too frequently, Barbara would be pulled over by a "baby boy cop" (her description) and lectured about driving 35 miles per hour in a school zone or, in this case, 20 miles per hour in a grocery store parking lot. She smilingly received her ticket, assured the "baby boy cop" of her desire for him to have a great day, and then raced off to her destination.

As Barbara waited to hand over her "racing money," the baby boy cop who had ticketed her walked through the door. Barbara jumped up and warmly said, "Well, there you are. Do you remember me? You gave me a ticket for driving too fast in the Albertson's parking lot yesterday."

He looked surprised and then suspicious. "Why don't you just mail the money for your fine? You don't have to come to the police station."

Barbara cheerfully told him if she mailed the money, she'd miss the fun of personally delivering the five-pound bag of See's Candy she had brought for everyone working in the department.

Then she winked at the baby boy cop, squeezed his hand, and said, "The world needs to be protected from people like me. So go ahead, have a chocolate butter cream and just know I appreciate you doing your job!"

Barbara not only helped me with my present, but she also contributed to my future. When Steve Arterburn "hatched" the idea of starting a women's conference, he asked for Barbara's advice about who might be the fourth speaker. Patsy Clairmont, Luci Swindoll, and Barbara had agreed to give the "little" conference a try, but Steve needed one more person. Barbara told him she had all my tapes and listened to them over and over because "she makes me laugh." He was concerned about my lack of national name recognition, but based on Barbara's high recommendation, he invited me to join the merry band of four speakers. There were no guest musicians, dramatists, or guest speakers. Originally the conference was called Laughing Ladies and then Joyful Journey and finally Women of Faith. It has been my "joyful privilege" to continue with Women of Faith into its twelfth year. Thank you, Barbara . . . thank you, Jesus.

Now that Barb is in heaven, I can imagine the scores of people who are there because of her faithful witness of God's love and grace. I also have a private giggle over the possibility of her having an autograph table where she can squeeze hands and say to each beaming face, "You're okay . . .you've come to right place."

## 44

# The Unforgettable Barbara Johnson

~ Luci Swindoll ~

The story goes that when Victor Hugo wanted to know how his book *Les Miserables* was selling, he telegraphed the publisher with the simple inquiry, "?". And almost by return mail he received the reply, "!".

One could say the same thing about the book sales of Barbara Johnson. They were "!", "!!", and "!!!!!" A prolific writer, Barbara broke all records as the best-selling Christian female author for years. Her books flew off the shelves. All of us were buying them, reading them, and passing them on to our friends. They were easy reads—full of fun, common sense, and helpful hints that encouraged us to look at the bright side of life, even when we wanted to throw in the towel or worse—crawl under the house and stay there for months. She spread joy wherever she went, and on her darkest days she imparted some of her best wisdom.

I also got her "Spatula Newsletter" each month and would often cut something out of it to stick in my journal: a word of tenderness, a joke, a cartoon . . . even a recipe for having a happy day. Barbara was famous for one-liners that gave us all a kick-start when we might be down or in a tough spot.

What you may not know is that Barbara Johnson was also a singer. She never wrote a hymnbook, but she did steal one. I know that for a fact because I have it. About ten years ago, she gave me a copy of *The Celebration Hymnal: Songs and Hymns for Worship* for my birthday. On front, she taped this little note, along with a geranium sticker:

> *The Celebration Hymnal* has all the pages turned down that I thought you would enjoy. I wanted you to know that these turned-down pages are my selections for you. It took time to go through this book because I wanted to *sing* every song that I had indicated was special.

Then, the last line of that note read, "Old hymnals are hard to find—unless you steal them!" There are sixty-one corners turned down throughout that stolen hymnal. Oh, and with that present, she also gave me two cassette tapes with the orchestral background of these very hymns, so that I could play them in my car as I drove along and sing the alto part . . . even if I didn't have a soprano anywhere nearby. What fun!

Every Friday night, the Women of Faith team has a special time of prayer in the greenroom before any of us goes onstage that first conference evening. It was very common when Women of Faith began in 1996 that we'd sing hymns during that time as well. We might sing five or six oldies that all of us loved and had learned in childhood. It was just the core team, singing and praying. And of course if we had enough people to carry the lead, Barb and I would sing harmony. I can hear it now in my head. What wonderful memories those are.

Once Barb learned of my love for music and growing-up years of singing the hymns of the faith, she gave me the hymnbook and tapes containing all those songs we mutually loved, so we could spend our days and meetings singing harmony together. She was an alto, like I. But most of the time I'd take the tenor line so we'd have even more harmony.

I remember one such occasion (apart from our Friday night worship times) when this happened. Barbara and I were both living in Southern California, and I was driving her to a Women of Faith gathering. Out of the blue she asked if I had those cassette tapes in the car. Well, indeed I did. I put one in the player, and together we had a hymn fest. We sang "Glory to His Name," "I Love to Tell the Story," "Revive Us Again," "My Savior's Love," and four or five others. But here's what's funny—we let the orchestra part do the lead and Barb sang alto while I sang tenor. Only the cassette tape was carrying the melody. What fun that was! Just singing our little hearts out as we drove along. Not conversing. Not visiting. Not talking about our schedules or our troubles . . . but just singing, singing, singing. Oh, I'll never forget that day! It was like there was no tomorrow with both of us lost in the wonder of those old hymns.

I had forgotten this, but I noticed the other day that Barbara had affixed to one of those turned-down page corners a little marker signifying it was one of her favorites. It was on the hymn "Grace Greater Than Our Sin." I stopped what I was doing and sang each verse, sort of in her honor. It felt good to sing and think about God's grace that is greater than our sins. And when I got to the last verse, I pondered the words especially—

> Marvelous, infinite, matchless grace,
> Freely bestowed on all who believe!
> You who are longing to see His face,
> Will you this moment His grace receive?

Somewhere in heaven, Barbara Johnson is enjoying this matchless, marvelous, infinite grace to the full. She trusted in the God who extends it, and she spent most of her life passing it on to others . . . writing, speaking and singing about it. I'm so glad to have known her and to have had a small part in her life. She left an enormous legacy of compassion, unselfishness, love, and grace to all of us, and now, when I hear that song, I smile in remembrance.

Barbara Johnson was a one-of-a-kind girlfriend. But her contagious joy, extravagant grace, irrepressible hope, and sense of adventure gave her a sensational life and made her everybody's friend. It's a joy to write about her and to relive some of these sweet memories.

*Barb, you deserve the biggest "!" ever.*

# Notes

1. John Rogers, "No Fading Star: Actress Gets Roles at 97," Associated Press article, 31 March 2007, available at http://www.usatoday.com/life/television/2007-03-29-3046814352_x.htm. Accessed 11 August 2007.
2. Victor Hugo, *Les Miserables,* Wordsworth Classics, vol. 2 (Lincolnwood, IL: NTC/Contemporary Publishing, 1997), 905.
3. John Rogers, "No Fading Star: Actress Gets Roles at 97."
4. Ibid.
5. "Surgery Removes Electric Blanket from Python," Associated Press article, 21 July 2006, available at http://www.msnbc.msn.com/id/13939272/. Accessed 11 August 2007.
6. For more information about Abounding Love Ministries, see www.aboundinglove.org.
7. United Negro College Fund, "Who We Are: The UNCF Brand," http://www.uncf.org/aboutus/branding.asp. Accessed 11 August 2007.
8. This story is told in more detail in Carol Kent's, *A New Kind of Normal* (Nashville: Thomas Nelson, 2007).
9. Edith Wharton, "The Fulness of Life," available at http://www.online-literature.com/wharton/2066/. Accessed 11 August 2007.
10. Charles Swindoll, *Grace Awakening* (Dallas: Word, 1990).
11. For more information about the judgment seat of Christ, see Erwin W. Lutzer, *Your Eternal Reward: Triumph and Tears at the Judgment Seat of Christ* (Chicago: Moody, 1998).
12. Rick Howard and Jamie Lash, *This Was Your Life: Preparing to Meet God Face to Face* (Grand Rapids: Chosen, 1998).
13. Charles Spurgeon, *Morning and Evening,* rev. ed. (New Kensington, PA: Whitaker House, 2001), 268: May 16, morning.

# WOMEN OF FAITH®

Women of Faith, North America's largest women's conference, is an experience like no other. Thousands of women — all ages, sizes, and backgrounds — come together in arenas for a weekend of love and laughter, stories and encouragement, drama, music, and more. The message is simple. The result is life-changing.

*What this conference did for me was to show me how to celebrate being a woman, mother, daughter, grandmother, sister or friend.*
*— Anne, Corona, CA*

*I appreciate how genuine each speaker was and that they were open and honest about stories in their life   even the difficult ones.*
*— Amy, Fort Worth, TX*

*GO, you MUST go.  The Women of Faith team is wonderful, uplifting, funny, blessed. Don t miss out on a chance to have your life changed by this incredible experience.*
*— Susan, Hartford, CT*